NOBODY'S WARRIORS

NOBODY'S WARRIORS

I.C. Modrick

PENTLAND PRESS, INC.
ENGLAND • USA • SCOTLAND

PUBLISHED BY PENTLAND PRESS, INC.

5124 Bur Oak Circle, Raleigh, North Carolina 27612
United States of America
919-782-0281

ISBN 1-57197-034-7
Library of Congress Catalog Card Number 96-69085

This is a work of fiction. Names, places, incidents and characters either are used fictitiously or are products of the author's imagination. Any resemblance to actual events or places or persons, living or dead, is merely coincidental.

Printed in the United States of America

"Ye shall know the truth and the truth will set you free."

This book is dedicated to the men who fought in the Vietnam War, to those who died, to those who lived and returned to the United States, and to those for whom the war has not ended, the prisoners of war. This book is for all those guys that have been tortured with memories and have been trying to let go. The people that we fought for need to know this is what it was like. We're not cry babies. We're not cowards. This is what we saw and what we and our buddies lived through. This was real.

FOREWORD

A hard-hitting action packed no holds barred account of the fighting men in Vietnam, *Nobody's Warriors*, with machine gun burst action describes mission after mission, each as terrifying and real as the last. The men come alive as their feelings and character—honor, cowardice, camaraderie, stupidity, heroism, insanity, outrage, humor—are captured with intensity. The novel is riveting and eye opening as our men confront horror, inhuman brutality, unspeakable cruelty.

Horrifying incidents are portrayed with disturbing realism, making *Nobody's Warriors* a "must read" for all those involved with Vietnam—those who served, those who were touched by the war, those who knew anyone who served and those who protested.

With the action and dialogue of a movie, the novel is easy to read and understand. *Nobody's Warriors* is a powerful picture of the Vietnam War and belongs in every high school and college library.

This moving and disturbing account is a testament to our fighting men in Vietnam. Those men were fallible and not perfect. Yet the majority overcame their fallibility, their ineptness, to rally together as one force united with just purpose ringing in their minds and hearts: meet the call of their country to duty, even to death.

The ones who lived returned home to a country which had rejected them. They were *Nobody's Warriors*. *Nobody's Warriors* is America!

Jim Zalar
Superintendent of Schools
Carmichaels Area School District

ACKNOWLEDGEMENTS

To my wife, Patty, without whose encouragement, patience, understanding, talents and love this book would never have been written.

To my son Carl, may he never know the horror of war.

To Jim and Shirley Zalar, whose encouragement for many years to write lit the flame that became *Nobody's Warriors*.

To "Bitta" Keller, a loyal friend.

To Suzanne Pletcher for all her help from inception to completion.

To our daughter Lisa, who never really cared about the book, but who loved her daddy and cared about him.

To three of my Leatherneck buddies who are guarding the "streets of Heaven": Jim Caputo, Jim Ryan, Jr., Mike Cvetan. I'm looking forward to the day that we again sing the Marine Corps Hymn together and with the angels.

May God bless you all!

AUGUST 1966 VIETNAM

The first night "in country" was so dark and so hot that some of the men tried to hide in it and others choked in it. There was an air of false bravado from some of the young and not-so-young Marines and quiet confidence from others. Some of the men were anxious for their baptism of fire; others prayed they would never see a shot fired in anger or have to fire one.

It was the first night for this company, mostly made up of Marines who had just arrived from the States, to actually be on a patrol. The company held up in a series of rice paddies in an L-shaped configuration. Two platoons were in the rice paddies closest to the jungle tree line and one platoon was behind in another rice paddy.

All they could see were the stars in the sky. There was no artificial light in any direction. When they looked toward the jungle they could make out the tree line, but no distinct figures or shapes of trees. They had to be within arm's length to see each other. It was ominously quiet. The only sounds to be heard were their occasional clankings and the noises of animals or birds from the jungle.

Some men were lying against the dikes of the rice paddies trying to peer into the jungle. Others were lying with their backs to the dikes in an effort to relax. A few sat trying to heat water for coffee in their empty C ration cans.

No one was comfortable. Everyone was nervous. Even though watches had been set up, almost everyone was at their watch position, those who were on duty and those who were not due to go on for four more hours. No one could sleep, anticipating the action most thought they craved.

One of the men glanced at his watch. It was 0330 (3:30 A.M.) and the quiet hung forebodingly in the atmosphere.

Suddenly mortars started falling among the Marines. There were bursts and flashes of blinding light. Deafening noise crashed everywhere around them. Terrified, panic and fear overtook most of them, and confusion reigned everywhere. Shocked by the suddenness of it, even the seasoned veterans were taken aback for a few seconds.

In the eruptions of light, men could be seen huddling against the dikes for protection, trying to curl themselves up into fetal positions to make themselves smaller.

Someone yelled, "Incoming! Hit the deck!"

Mortars landed outside of the positions. Others that fell inside the Marine perimeter hit their mark and caused casualties. The air was filled with moans and screams of pain. Some of the men started firing aimlessly. Others screamed for the corpsmen. A few didn't know whether to shit or go blind.

Some of the N.C.O.s yelled, "Get to your positions and stay down, Marines!" Others screamed, "Fields of fire! Fields of fire!" (telling the Marines to fire in their predesignated areas) although there was nothing to fire at. After a few disorganized moments the N.C.O.s got the men under control and to their proper positions.

A brief silence . . . and again the mortars rained down on them.

Captain Raye, company commander, called for Gunnery Sergeant Clarke (known as Alley Oop, or Oop for short).

"Get me Oop up here!"

Several hand-fired flares had stuck in trees and gave the Marines some light, but the V.C. were still invisible. Eyes narrowed and brows knitted, Captain Raye looked over the situation and assessed his next move. Raye had a chiseled look about him. He was on the thin side, and had a sharp chin, brown eyes and a slightly hawkish nose. His brown hair was cropped Marine short. Oop came running to where the captain was set up to the side of one of the front rice paddies.

Oop (Gunnery Sergeant Clarke) was a poster Marine. Just under six feet tall, he had a broad chest, narrow waist, square jaw, dark hair, and dark eyes that could look through you or cut you down to size. And, when he was in the mood, a flashing smile and an infectious laugh. Oop had been an advisor prior to American troops being committed to combat and was salty and knowledgeable . . . born for combat.

"Yes, sir?"

"Oop," Captain Raye said, "I want you to take a squad and see if you can find where those mortars are coming from."

Oop said, "Yes, sir. Issue the order to the platoon guarding that area so we don't get in a firefight with each other."

The mortars stopped. Almost immediately women's voices came from the rear of the Marines' position.

"Marine no shoot! Marine no shoot! We no V.C.!"

Oop had started to turn away to get his men to silence the mortars, but he stopped when he heard the voices. He turned to the captain and said, "Don't let anyone inside the perimeter . . . no one, Captain!"

He turned, left the command post, got his men and moved out of the perimeter into the night. Before the captain could spread the word not to let anyone inside the perimeter his radio cracked to life and his radio man said, "Captain, Lieutenant Fenig for you, sir."

Lieutenant Fenig was a young overbearing officer who had not won the respect of his men mainly because of an attitude that he was superior to them not only in rank but in every way. Fenig, with blond hair and green eyes, was a typical pretty boy who looked down his nose at everyone. He always displayed this arrogance about him, so that ninety percent of the people who met him instantly disliked him and his conceited, overbearing attitude.

Before responding to Fenig, Captain Raye addressed his radio man. "Get the platoon commanders on the horn," he instructed.

Raye picked up the hand set. "I want you to get your wounded out so that the choppers can evac them," he ordered. "Lieutenant Fenig, you send a squad of men to move the wounded back to the clearing in your position. Over." (This was done so the corpsmen would have a more concentrated area so that they could treat the wounded men more quickly.)

Lieutenant Kezell, commander of the far platoon, replied, "Roger, out."

Fenig, commander of the near platoon, informed the captain, "Sir, I have already allowed Vietnamese nationals inside my perimeter. I have twelve women and six children. I took them in to protect them."

The captain, remembering Oop's warning, shook his head with a frown and said, "Keep an eye on them! And get our wounded settled in. There won't be any choppers until daylight. Out."

Oop and his men arrived at the far left corner of the Marine defensive perimeter. To the sergeant in charge he said, "I'm going to take a squad about a hundred meters to your left, then move into the tree line. Have your men hold their fire. We'll stay in touch by radio."

The platoon sergeant of the defensive perimeter nodded and said, "Good hunting." Oop and his men were off into the night.

The squad was well trained and organized. They moved quickly and silently through the dry rice paddies and into the jungle. Their surroundings changed immediately from open ground to dense jungle growth. It was black as a hole to hell in the dense underbrush and it slowed them down considerably as they attempted to remain quiet.

The point man (the lead assigned for lookout) stopped and passed the word back for Oop to come up front. When Oop got to him they both listened intently. They could hear faint metallic sounds.

Oop said, "They're breaking down the mortars."

He quickly called the squad.

"Move quick and quiet. Anything moves, shoot it. Let's go."

They moved stealthily to the edge of the clearing where the mortars were being carried away. The squad spread out and opened fire. Oop fired a hand-held flare after the firing started so that the men could see what they were shooting. They could see that most of the V.C. had moved out. They ceased fire and moved to gather the bodies of the four V.C. K.I.A.s (kills) and the two complete mortars which they had taken in the attack.

Oop's second in command, "Mad Dog" Matthews, approached Oop. Mad Dog was a big man, dark-haired, dark-skinned, powerful and broad-shouldered. He had the confident, assured presence of a professional boxer or football player. Fearless, tough and quick-thinking, able to move with the speed of a cat, he was an unrelenting warrior, and he looked it. Mad Dog had served with Oop in an advisory position earlier in Vietnam. Together they made a fearsome pair.

"Oop," he said, "I have the men in temporary defensive positions. They could have lobbed shit on us all night by just moving and having a listening post on each side. What the hell's going on?"

Oop didn't answer. He immediately called his radio man. "Raise the C.P. quick!"

The radio man got the C.P. Oop took the handset and spoke to the C.O. (code name, Boxer). "Boxer, this is Boxer 44. We're in temporary defensive positions. They've faded into the jungle. Don't let those women and children inside the perimeter! Over."

The C.O. answered back, "They're in, but we're watching them. Over."

Oop came back, "Put them out, Boxer!!! Over."

The C.O. came back, "Roger, out."

The sun was just starting to rise as Oop and his men left the cover of the jungle. They had radioed ahead so that the Marines would not open fire at their movement. They had the four dead V.C. and the mortars with them. Oop had requested a squad of Marines to come out to carry the bodies and the mortars.

As the relief squad moved into the jungle to meet Oop's men, Captain Raye ordered that other troops prepare and be ready to load the wounded and the dead onto the medevac choppers. He sent several men on ahead to prepare the wounded. Then, every-thing in order, Captain Raye, his radio man, and the other men he had gathered went to the area where Lieutenant Fenig had put the wounded the previous night.

As they neared the area, Captain Raye and the others heard wails and screams of, "Oh my God!!! Oh God, no!!! Noooo!!!!" They ran up to the clearing and stopped dead in their tracks. Before them was a grisly sight.

The Marines who had been wounded the night before and the corpsmen who had been nursing them, lay in bloody twisted shapes. All of their throats were cut. The women and children that Lieutenant Fenig had taken in for protection, had slit their throats, stripped their jewelry, and taken their weapons and medical supplies. It was obvious by the positions of the bodies that some of the men had struggled when they realized what was being done to them. The women and children, stealing off with-out a sound, had disappeared into the jungle.

The sight was so shocking that some of the men began to throw up. The captain immediately called choppers in to evacu-ate the dead Marines. Soon the paddle sounds of the arriving helicopters filled the air. The Marines looked at the bodies in horror and at Lieutenant Fenig in disgust.

WATER BUFFALO
INCIDENT

As the choppers were lifting off with the dead Marines, the corpsmen and the captured V.C. mortars, Captain Raye was called to the radio. He was given orders to rendezvous approximately three clicks south near a Viet Cong village. Raye called for his officers and staff N.C.O.'s to inform them that they would be walking the three clicks to the village and then transported to headquarters on choppers.

The Marines spread out and started walking in the direction of the village. The terrain they were crossing was mostly dry rice paddies and occasional small streams. The men, faces drawn and angry, walked in brooding silence. Low curses and "stupid motherfucker" were heard darkly mumbled from the troops. No one needed to ask who the obscenities were directed at. Lieutenant Fenig knew also, and made mental notes of who said what.

As they neared the village, several men suddenly fell to their knees screaming in agony. Punji sticks had ripped through their feet and out the tops of their boots. The men, startled, scattered about, several more taking the spikes in their feet. (Punji sticks were sharpened metal or bamboo spikes buried in camouflaged holes so that when someone stepped on them the spike ran through their foot. There were also larger versions of these used to impale American bodies.)

Mad Dog screamed, "Don't move, you dumb shits!!! Stay where you are until we check this whole area for booby traps!"

Mad Dog and several of his men started to probe the earth with their bayonets as the men who were wounded groaned in pain. No one spoke as two of the men started to probe with precision in the direction of the wounded and two others started in the middle of the paddy. They found two grenades triggered to go off when pressure was applied and disarmed them, and three more punjis.

The in-battle Marines had all been issued old style boots . . . ones with no metal inserts, so they had no protection against this type of injury except to watch carefully where they stepped.

The choppers landed and they began loading men, including the men injured by the punji sticks. One Marine had a particularly bad wound. The punji stick, deep in his foot, had been imbedded in cement. The in-line Marines had no bolt cutters to cut off the spike, so the whole thing had to be dug up and moved with his foot. The wounded Marine had to be laid on a stretcher with the spike, cement block and all, still attached, until he could be gotten to a main hospital where they would have the necessary equipment to remove the block and take the spike out.

The relief company commanding officer met Captain Raye and requested a briefing. Captain Raye had several officers with him, including some staff noncommissioned officers; the same applied to the relief company commander. Captain Raye addressed the relief company commander.

"Gunnery Sergeant Clarke was an advisor and has a lot of experience dealing with the Vietnamese. I think it would be better if I let him describe the situation to you rather than me."

Oop said, "The first thing you have to learn, Captain, is these people have absolutely no respect for life. They . . . "

Fenig, obviously meaning to be center stage, interrupted him. "Gunny," he sneered, "you don't know that for sure."

Captain Raye looked at Fenig and said, "At ease, Lieutenant." He turned to Oop and said, "Would you please continue, Gunny."

Then Gunny said, "They wave at you in the day and smile, and they come out to kill you at night."

Fenig again interrupted. "No one was waving at us in the day."

Captain Raye looked at him again as did all the officers and N.C.O.s in the small group.

Raye dryly said, "At ease, Lieutenant. When your vast knowledge of the Viet Cong and their tactics is needed, I'll use your expertise. Right now, Oop's is needed—and wanted—understand?"

Just then Oop looked up. It was almost a sixth sense with him. He saw a young girl of twelve or thirteen on a water buffalo with a case of soda pop in glass bottles strapped to each side flat out on the water buffalo. She called to the Marines and offered them a cool bottle of pop.

Oop sprang to his feet and started running and screaming.

"No! Stop!!! Get away!!!"

The girl looked up, then slammed her hand into her chest.

A violent explosion . . . glass . . . blood . . . guts . . . brains . . . flew everywhere. She was disintegrated. Two hoofs and the buffalo's head landed in the mire. Seventeen Marines were decimated. Thirty-six others were wounded and blinded by the explosion and the glass shards. Moaning, crying, screams of agony and men calling for corpsmen filled the air. Some of the men, in useless reaction, set up defensive perimeters.

Oop turned around and yelled to the captain, "Get choppers here quick, skipper!" He ran toward the wounded and dead.

"Dog, get over here!" he yelled. He didn't have to call. Dog was already moving with his squad on the double to the carnage and the decimated wounded.

A Vietnamese man and woman came running toward where the explosion had happened, screaming and crying and wringing their hands. The Marine's interpreter stopped them. After he had finished talking to them, the interpreter, speaking more to Oop and Mad Dog than to the officers, described what had happened.

"The Viet Cong told her that this would help her to attract the Marines to buy her pop. They wrapped her in C-4 (a plastic explosive) and didn't tell the girl or her family what it was. She was just to get as many Marines around her as possible and hit the button (detonator) on her chest. The family had no idea what would happen. They thought she was lucky to make some money selling pop. And obviously she never knew what hit her."

The total horror of what they were seeing and had just heard caused many of the relief troops to back away. Several fell and crawled backwards on their rears and hands for a few feet, then just sat in horror. N.C.O.s and officers moved to help them regain their composure and regrouped the decimated company.

Oop, Mad Dog and their men worked among the wounded to patch them up. They moved the dead to one area, doing their best to comfort and help the critically wounded. For a brief period they were the only organized unit other than the men who had set up the useless defense perimeter.

Again the choppers came. This time to take the entire company to headquarters.

JUNGLE GEAR

The choppers landed. Captain Raye and all the officers reported to Colonel Tartus, the battalion commander. As they approached the command post they noted with utter disdain the mailman leaving the command post pressed out in "jungle utilities" and "jungle boots."

They entered the colonel's office which was actually a large tent. There were also several other officers awaiting their arrival. Among them was Colonel Larry Fike, an aide to the commanding general of all the Marine forces. Captain Raye gave his report of casualties.

Colonel Tartus asked, "Did you get a body count in the first encounter?"

"No, sir," Captain Raye answered.

"Why?" the colonel retorted.

"Colonel, my first obligation was to protect our company. We couldn't see in the jungle, and I didn't want to lose men just trying to count gook bodies in the dead of night."

"Captain, you know how important a body count is when we have to make our reports. In the future I want a body count, is that clear?"

"Yes, Colonel. May I go on?"

"Proceed."

"Colonel Tartus, my men need jungle boots and utilities. We have unnecessary casualties because we don't have the proper equipment. I had several men step on punjis on the march here. This kind of unnecessary injury could be avoided if the men had the proper footwear."

Tartus replied, "This issue is one of my top priorities for the entire battalion, but my supplies are limited."

Colonel Tartus and, indeed, all of the headquarters personnel were, however, wearing jungle outfits. (This did not escape Colonel Fike and being the type of officer and Marine he was, it made him feel very uncomfortable.)

In the reporting of what took place it became obvious that the battalion commander, Colonel Tartus, was partial to Lieutenant Fenig, and made sure he was included in all discussions.

After Captain Raye had given his report on the incident concerning the wounded who had been murdered, Colonel Tartus turned to Fenig and asked, "Lieutenant Fenig, what were your observations about this operation?"

Fenig answered, "Colonel, I had my area secure. I don't know who was supposed to be watching those Vietnamese nationals."

Captain Raye interrupted him, more out of embarrassment for the young lieutenant than anything else. The other officers, other than Colonel Tartus, were disgusted by Fenig's very obvious bullshit excuse.

"Lieutenant Fenig. Let's get on with the business at hand."

He turned to the others. "I suggest we call in Gunnery Sergeant Clarke for some in-depth knowledge on what's happening here. The Oop has experience as an advisor and can give us some insight in this situation through his experience with the Vietnamese."

The whining Lieutenant Fenig, totally ignoring protocol, interjected, "We don't need an enlisted man's opinion."

Colonel Tartus inserted, "I agree. We officers don't need any advice from enlisted men."

Another colonel who was observing for the general cut in to say, "I personally know the Oop. I've been offering him a commission for years. I, for one, would be interested in listening to

what he has to say, Lieutenant. And I'm sure most of these officers in this room will learn from him."

Colonel Tartus was taken aback. He spoke, with just a hint of
resentment in his voice. "We all could learn from experience and
Gunnery Sergeant Clarke certainly has a lot of experience with
the Vietnamese."

Oop was called in. Colonel Fike and several of the other officers got up and warmly shook hands with him. Colonel Fike,
smiling, spoke.

"It's a real pleasure to see you again, Gunnery Sergeant
Clarke. We're interested in your assessment of the Vietnamese
and the recent occurrences."

Dog, obviously uncomfortable, said, "The Marines should be
kept away from the Vietnamese and the villages in the field
unless they are objects of a search and destroy mission. We're
getting killed and we don't know who the enemy is."

Lieutenant Fenig, ignoring protocol, interjected with, "We
know who the enemy is, Sergeant. Don't you?"

Mad Dog, his dark eyes flashing, looked at the lieutenant
with disgust and hatred. He took a breath, but before he could
speak, Oop interjected with acid bitterness.

"Like you knew the women and kids were the enemy,
Lieutenant?"

Fenig's mouth dropped open. His lips moved, but no sound
came out.

Colonel Fike took over. "My reason for being here is to ask
Oop to volunteer for a squad-sized reconnaissance mission. As
you know, normally a reconnaissance mission doesn't require
such a large contingent of men. There may be accidental contact.
I want my men protected as best as possible. I have permission
to use you, Oop, but I'd prefer it if you'd volunteer because it is
such a dangerous mission."

"I volunteer. Can I pick my men?"

As the officer in charge of the men, Colonel Tartus spoke up.
"Of course," he said, trying to sound congenial.

Oop turned to Mad Dog. "Dog, get twelve more men."

Dog left. Lieutenant Fenig, always trying to be center stage,
turned to Oop.

"Why didn't you tell him not to say anything about your mission?"

Oop closed his eyes slowly and stood, not speaking, for a moment. Then he opened his eyes, and with a look of controlled patience, spoke.

"Lieutenant: One, I trust him. Two, we really don't know anything yet. Three, if you would relax you could learn a lot from the Dog. He has instincts that are uncanny and it'll save a lot of Marines' lives if we use him right."

Fenig totally ignored Oop and looked at Colonel Fike. "I'd like to volunteer to be in charge of this mission, sir."

Colonel Fike couldn't completely mask his disgust. "The Oop is in charge, Lieutenant. This is too small an operation to send more men or officers."

Lieutenant Fenig opened his mouth to protest, but Colonel Fike raised his hand. Lieutenant Fenig wisely shut up.

"Oop," Colonel Fike said, "meet me in my office in an hour with Sergeant Matthews."

The meeting over, Colonel Fike immediately headed for supply.

"I want to see the officer in charge," he said.

A first lieutenant emerged pressed out in his jungle utilities and, of course, wearing the jungle boots.

Colonel Fike said, "Lieutenant, are we having a problem getting jungle gear to our line troops?"

"Well, Colonel," was the pompous reply, "I have my orders from higher up to issue these clothes cautiously. I can't just give them to everybody."

"Let me see your supply of jungle gear, Lieutenant."

"I have plenty of jungle gear, but I have to have proper authorization in my chain of command to issue it."

With a look of disgust on his face, the colonel held up his hand, walked over to the phone and picked it up.

"This is Colonel Fike. Get the general for me, please."

The supply lieutenant's eyes opened wide. He almost shit his trousers.

"General, this is Colonel Fike. General, some of our line companies are without proper jungle gear and we have a warehouse full of it. The O.I.C. here tells me it is a question of authorization."

After a brief pause, he said, "Yes, sir," and hung up the phone.

"Lieutenant, you're on notice as of now, to outfit every line company until the gear is exhausted. Now go with Major Binner and take care of these men immediately."

The enlisted men present, who had witnessed this entire scene, smiled at their O.I.C.'s obvious discomfort.

Major Binner left with the lieutenant and took him to Oop. "This is the officer in charge of supplies," he said.

Oop nodded.

"Lieutenant, you are to issue jungle clothing and boots immediately to all the men that Gunnery Sergeant Clarke designates. Take care of this right now."

"Yes, sir," the lieutenant answered.

The outfits that had been needed months before were issued at last.

PUFF THE MAGIC DRAGON

Oop and Mad Dog arrived at the colonel's office where they were briefed on what they were to look for.

"I suspect there is an extension of the Ho Chi Minh Trail that is sending supplies to the south. My guess is that North Vietnamese regulars are moving to the south to aid the V.C. by pretending to be V.C. rather than N.V.A. I want you to take the recon patrol and go in there to have a look," the colonel concluded.

Mad Dog had already chosen the twelve men and they soon were loaded into two choppers and headed north. When the choppers approached the hill that Oop and his men were to observe from, they began a cat and mouse routine of darting into the valleys and rising. They swooped down and only landed long enough for the men to jump out. Even after Oop and his men were away, the choppers continued the cat and mouse game to offer protection for the small recon patrol.

The patrol grouped and started to climb the hill. Oop and Mad Dog had cautioned them separately that quietness was extremely important. Not knowing what they would encounter, and with so few of them, it was their only protection.

As total night fell, the patrol was in place on the top of an obscure hill only identified by a number. (Vietnamese hills were normally numbered by their height in meters.) Oop assigned four men to stay awake and told the others to "crap out." They'd be awakened later for their watch.

He called Dog over to where he stood. "This is touchier than I expected," he said. "Take three men and recon the valley."

Dog got three men and left. The four Marines crept quietly down the hill to the bank of a small river. Almost immediately a group of unsuspecting N.V.A.s came to the river for water. They were talking naturally, not suspecting they were being watched from the opposite side of the stream. The N.V.A.s grab-assed and laughed and chattered to each other as more men kept coming for water.

Dog signaled his men to return to the hilltop. Meanwhile he waited to see how many North Vietnamese he would see. After over an hour he crept back and away to the top of the hill. All the while the North Vietnamese were unaware of his presence and were laughing and joking and talking normally. Dog got back and reported to Oop.

"There is at least one N.V.A. division just on the other side of the river. Call in the air and blast their asses off."

Oop raised the headquarters of special operations and gave coded positions of the North Vietnamese.

He was told, "No air strikes until daybreak."

Just as the sun came up, the men who had the watch called Oop and Dog. In the valley crossing the river were swarms of North Vietnamese army regulars. Oop immediately radioed a request for air strikes. He also requested "Puff the Magic Dragon" and choppers to take his men out.

The choppers were sent from the small airstrip at Dong Ha. Unfortunately, one of them had engine problems and turned back. Only nine men could get on the one that arrived. The remaining men would have to be left behind. Oop, Dog and three others stayed. Their only choice was to use the radio to direct fire and hope that another chopper could make it before the enemy closed in.

The chopper pilot had seen the N.V.A.s. As soon as the men were on board, he took off and turned sharply to fly back the same way he had come in to avoid ground fire from the N.V.A.

He radioed back to base in plain language, "We only had one chopper. Get the jets here and move it—some of our men are still in there! Out."

The N.V.A. quickly surrounded the hill, and not knowing how many men were on the top, began to slowly tighten the noose on the five Marines. Just as the jets arrived, the Marines saw the first of the N.V.A.s approach their position.

Oop radioed, "They're almost on us . . . no more than twenty or thirty meters away from us on all sides. Put it on us. We can't get out. Better to bite it from you fly guys than the Gooks! Out."

Two F-4s came screaming in from the north, one flying southeast, the other flying southwest to clear the hill. Two more came directly from the south targeting the bottom of the hill in an attempt to blast a path for the Marines to run through. Napalm exploded and fires raged.

Just then, "Puff" arrived.

"Puff on station. Where do you want me to dump my load?"

The voice of the chopper pilot that had been ordered in from another airfield came through to Oop next: "Boxer 44, follow Puff's fire down the hill and your daddy will be there to pick you up," he drawled matter-of-factly.

Puff, the beautiful old son of a bitch, banked to the left to give the most effective cover fire for the trapped Marines. She spewed her deadly cargo—a bullet hit every two inches and she could cover a football field.

Oop looked at his men and grinned, "Chalk up a bunch for the US Air Force!" And almost as an afterthought, "Let's go!!!"

The five Marines were on their feet and tearing down the hill screaming like refugees from a banshee insane asylum. They jumped over dead commie bodies and equipment, Oop leading the way and Mad Dog in the rear.

The choppers swooped in low. The gunners were alert for any movement other than the five Marines, while the pilot, copilot and gunners cheered them on loudly, inwardly saying silent prayers for their comrades.

With the chopper not touching down, the five Marines leaped and clawed themselves aboard while gunners left their position to pull them in. The five were huffing and puffing, laughing and crying uncontrollable tears of joy. Then, gratified silence . . . thanking God just to be alive.

The F-4s had regrouped in the air and were now diving with the remainder of their bombs to pound the Communist soldiers. Fire, explosions sending out blasts of earth, and the thunderous noise of the onslaught filled the air.

The chopper sped south to safety.

MOVING OUT

Things calmed down as they put miles between the chopper and the disaster. The crew chief turned to Oop and briefed him on the activities in the camp. The battalion had been ordered out and had been moved to Dong Ha that morning. They were waiting for Oop and his men there.

In Dong Ha, Captain Raye, Colonel Fike and several other officers were at the airstrip waiting for the rescue chopper. As Oop and his men dismounted the chopper the waiting officers noticed that all five were bleeding from superficial wounds. None of the five realized that they had been hit.

Colonel Fike ordered, "Get these men to the field hospital now!"

The five were too tired to protest. Oop and Mad Dog rode in the colonel's jeep with Captain Raye driving. The colonel turned in his seat and looked at Oop and Mad Dog.

"You men did a great job. There's going to be a medal in this for all of you."

Mad Dog replied, "Beggin' the colonel's pardon, my ass in one piece is the only medal I'm interested in!"

The four broke into gales of laughter. Captain Raye shook his head with a look of amazed wonder. "It's true! Mad Dog is a Marine's best friend!"

Colonel Fike waited with them as the men were patched up with merthiolate and a few bandages. The colonel, grinning, turned to look at Captain Raye.

"I'll bet you have a bottle hidden away for an event just like this," he said.

"I have a better deal than that," replied Raye. "Two cases of ice cold beer and a bottle of great Kentucky sippin' whiskey."

Oop looked wide-eyed at both officers.

"You'll make major yet, Captain!" he quipped.

The four retired to the captain's tent and he sent for the rest of the recon patrol to join them. Oop, Mad Dog, Captain Raye and the colonel guzzled their beer with relish. Surprisingly, most of the other Marines asked for soft drinks.

The next morning, Captain Raye had a meeting with his officers and N.C.O.s. "As soon as the entire battalion is at Dong Ha, we will be moving out to Cam Lo. It's a small village a few clicks down the road. We have the point company and will be setting up a camp for the general. He should be there in two days. This is going to be a major search and destroy operation." The meeting adjourned.

The next morning the battalion moved out in a motorized convoy. Oop had the point or lead jeep. He stopped the convoy at a bridge and got out of his jeep to inspect it. He walked across the bridge moving to the other side while Mad Dog and a few other Marines covered him. Just as Oop raised his hand to signal the convoy to proceed, Mad Dog spotted a cord running under the bridge.

"Hold it!!!" Mad Dog shouted while running toward the cord. Just as he reached to slash the cord with his K-bar, the N.V.A. spotted him. They detonated the charge. The force of the explosion sent parts of the bridge flying. Dog was blasted into the air and blown part way over the hill. He landed with a thump almost in a sitting position.

Mad Dog shook his head and, still in a daze, pulled the pins on his grenades and dropped them over the hill. The N.V.A.s came running out from their cover. Oop cut them down with three short bursts from his automatic weapon.

Then he yelled across the void, "Are you okay, Mad Dog?"

Mad Dog had regained his senses. "Oop, I think these gook motherfuckers are trying to kill me!"

Oop yelled back, "It wouldn't surprise me a bit!"

Two of the Marines who had been covering Oop looked at each other in amazement. One said, "I guess we know how they got their nicknames now!"

The other said, "I think they both escaped from the nut house!"

The bridge was temporarily repaired and the small convoy moved on.

CAM LO

As they arrived at Cam Lo a beautiful Eurasian woman was walking along the highway. She was neatly dressed in a clean pink outfit, not the usual dingy black pajamas that everyone in Vietnam seemed to wear. Some of the wilder young Marines, commenting on how good she looked to them, stopped and asked if she wanted a ride.

In perfect English she replied, "No, thank you," and kept on walking.

The battalion had set up just outside Cam Lo adjacent to an A.R.V.N. artillery battery and secured a large area for the general's headquarters. It was now their third day at Cam Lo.

Mad Dog, who was slightly sore and had several brush burns from his experience at the bridge, was on his way to get some topical medicine to keep his wounds from becoming infected. As he was walking, he noticed four Vietnamese running from behind the general's tent. He took off running through a graveyard to head them off.

Dog came around a grave mound one way and the four Vietnamese the other. He had surprised them. Their eyes registered total terror. One pulled a pistol. Dog shot him through the head before he could use it. Another slashed Dog with a knife. Dog fired two shots point blank into him. Dog knocked the third down with his rifle butt. The fourth tried to run away, but it was impossible to outrun the two quick shots snapped off by Dog that sent the Vietnamese to the not-so-happy hunting ground.

The one still living started chattering and clicking in the unintelligible way that Orientals do when they are excited, while his eyes bulged out in fear. He tried to reach into his shirt. Dog kicked him in the balls to calm him down. Oop came running on the double with several other Marines to lend assistance to Dog.

When the three dead and one live Vietnamese were searched, official situation reports for all the Marine operations were found on them. These reports told where each unit was located, each unit's strength, what casualties had occurred, and when and where they would be moving. It would have been totally devastating for these papers to have fallen into N.V.A. hands. They would have crucified the Marine companies on the operations noted on the reports.

The general had been advised about what had happened and the part Mad Dog had played with his quick thinking and quick actions. He personally told Mad Dog that he would see to it that Mad Dog be decorated for his bravery.

However, one of the general's aides—the one who had been originally assigned to destroy the situation reports—felt that if word got out that he had not properly disposed of the classified information he might be given a reprimand. When the papers from the general relaying the request for Mad Dog's decoration came to his desk, he rigged a way to quash the recommendation for the award. Then he perverted the report so that his friend Lieutenant Fenig was decorated. As many good officers and men know, this was not an uncommon practice.

THE ROCK PILE

Oop stood looking at the map studying the lay of the land around the "rock pile." The rock pile was just that . . . a natural outcropping of rocks in the midst of tangled jungle maze, sitting like a huge carelessly tossed stone haystack, several hundred feet high. Its only access was by helicopter.

"Mad Dog, the captain asked me to get together a squad of men to go to the rock pile on reconnaissance to protect Super Snoop Rofsky and his men. Want to go along?"

Oop looked up and gave Mad Dog a wry grin.

"Yeah, I'll go."

Mad Dog stood up and headed for the door. "I'll get the men together."

Mad Dog made the preparations and reported for the briefing. Oop was standing outside the commanding officer's tent. His expression was drawn and tense.

"There's been a change in plans," he said through clenched teeth. "Gunny Arno is taking my place. I know you can't stand him, so I'll talk to the skipper about getting you out of this."

"Thanks, Oop. I couldn't go with that son of a bitch! He smells like a billy goat, and is the biggest shit bird I ever saw. I don't know how in the hell he ever made gunny sergeant in this man's Marine Corps."

Just then a tall, somewhat pear-shaped Marine gunnery sergeant came strutting up. He looked and acted like a dyed-in-the-wool yahoo . . . a Gomer Pyle's father kind of character, one who was in constant need of a bath. Normally he was never trusted with any real responsibility, and was only given the most insignificant of work details. Somehow he had wormed his way into this detail. The officers in charge must have felt that no harm would come with Mad Dog as his assistant.

Arno was all smiles as he entered the C.O.'s tent, followed by Oop and Mad Dog.

"Requesting permission to speak to you in private," Oop said, speaking to the C.O.

"Sure," was the reply, and the captain and Oop stepped outside.

"Captain, Mad Dog volunteered because he thought that I would be leading this mission. I'm sure you know that he doesn't get along with Gunny Arno."

The captain kept a casual stance. "Oop," he replied, "you were my choice. The colonel sent word down that Arno was to lead this. I wish that Mad Dog would stay. I'd feel better about the men. And Rofsky specifically asked for you and Mad Dog. I think he'd be much happier with one or the other."

"Aye, aye, sir."

They turned and entered the tent being used as a command post. The captain started the briefing. Mad Dog looked at Oop. They looked square into each other's eyes. It was almost as though Mad Dog could read Oop's mind as the captain spoke.

" . . . and you'll be dropped off in choppers. You will be there to protect Sergeant Rofsky and his men and their equipment. The North Vietnamese may try to climb the rock pile to infiltrate. Their aim will be to destroy the equipment and or kill the men."

When the captain finished, Mad Dog spoke.

"Sir, I was told that Oop was going to be leading this mission and that's why I volunteered."

"Gunny Arno's in charge now," the captain replied. "I'd appreciate it if you would go along . . . so I won't have to make a lot of changes."

Mad Dog picked up on the captain's implication.

Arno, crestfallen, was looking downtrodden. He knew Mad Dog's reputation . . . he fought like a mad dog! He also knew that Mad Dog had the respect of the men . . . something that he himself did not.

Mad Dog replied tersely, "Yes, sir, Captain. I see your point. We'll still go. I believe I can speak for my men."

"That will be all, Gunny," the captain said, looking at Arno.

Arno came to attention and left. As soon as Arno was out of earshot, the captain spoke.

"Dog, I appreciate this. Do I have to explain my position?"

Mad Dog looked at the captain and waved his hand in dissension.

"I think I already know, Captain. I don't think I could respect myself if I let my men go out with him and I wasn't along."

"Thanks, Dog. You better get ready and mount up."

"Yes, sir."

Mad Dog turned and left the tent. Oop followed him out. As they walked back to where Mad Dog's gear was stowed, Oop made small talk.

"You better check in both with the company and battalion comm center and also with Rofsky's super snoop comm center when you're permitted in his area."

Mad Dog grabbed his gear and yelled at his men.

"Let's mount up!"

They walked to the chopper pad together. Rofsky and his men were already aboard with their equipment. Mad Dog and his men were to be dropped off first to secure the area. The choppers flew low, but couldn't land. They hovered a few feet over the rock pile while the Marines debarked the chopper. As soon as they were all on the ground, he had them spread out to the edges. It was rocky and tough going. He deployed the men away from where the choppers would be dropping Rofsky and his men on to the rocks.

The choppers that had dropped them off were soon out of the way and the ones with Rofsky and his men rapidly replaced them. One chopper circled as gun ship to protect the other as Rofsky, being the pro he was, smoothly and efficiently got his men and equipment off in short order. Fortunately all went well and the choppers were soon safely away.

Smiling, Mad Dog walked over to Rofsky. The two men had a certain bonding that had developed out of mutual respect. Rofsky, although he was almost pudgy and not the lean and mean kind of Marine, was the best at what he did. This electronics genius was super intelligent, yet he didn't look down at the other men, and Mad Dog respected that.

Rofsky had to set up certain of his equipment at a specific spot. After he took the measurements that were necessary, his men quickly got the direction finding equipment into place, and set up their other electronics gear. Then they pitched tents as best they could for some protection against the heat of the day and the mist and rain that frequently came in. The first few days were totally uneventful. Rofsky's men were busy, but there wasn't really much for Mad Dog and his men to do.

The men were sitting around the area quietly talking when suddenly mortars came raining in. Rofsky, who had been lounging and shooting the breeze with Mad Dog, dove behind some rocks. Mad Dog dove slightly at a right angle so that their feet were almost together, but they were protected by the rocks.

They weren't sure how many mortars hit . . . eight . . . ten . . . twelve. The mortars stopped. Mad Dog looked up.

"Oh shit, Rofsky, they hit some of your equipment."

They were both up and scrambling as best they could over the uneven ground to see if any of the men were hit. Two of Rofsky's men who had been operating the direction finder were dead. Both were unrecognizable. Mad Dog and Rofsky covered them in their ponchos, wrapped them and laid them down as best they could.

Just as they were finished the mortars started raining down again. Some of the men had heard Mad Dog and Rofsky and had started toward them to help. One of them was hit by the second or third mortar round that exploded.

Gunny Arno, who was a few feet away, saw the man hit and dove for cover. The man staggered and fell fully exposed on top of a rock. Mad Dog and Rofsky didn't hesitate. Both began to scramble feverishly over the rocks, any way they could to get to the injured man. It was only a short way, but it seemed like an eternity as everything seemed to be happening in slow motion.

They got the wounded Marine between rocks for cover and Rofsky dove on top of the Marine to protect him with his body, just as a mortar hit a few feet away. Fortunately it hit between two rocks, but it was enough of an explosion that it blew Mad Dog partially over the hill.

The starting and stopping of the mortar fire lasted for several hours. No one knew if Mad Dog was dead or alive. When the firing finally stopped, Rofsky checked his men and then shouted to Arno.

"Is Mad Dog okay?"

Arno, who hadn't come out of hiding yet, pretended not to hear, and didn't reply. Rofsky made his way over to the spot where Mad Dog had been blown over the hill.

"Mad Dog!!! Mad Dog!!! Are you okay?"

Mad Dog's voice came back unsteadily. "I'm busted up a little, Rofsky. But I'm okay. Can you get a line down to me?"

One of Mad Dog's men who had seen him blown over the side, came up with one of the mountain climbing ropes they had brought with them. He secured one end around himself and threw the rest of the rope to Rofsky.

"Put this around a rock and lower me down," he grunted.

A few other men who by this time had made their way to the spot grabbed the line and the Marine started down to Mad Dog.

Mad Dog looked up and saw the Marine on his way down.

"No, no!!! Just throw the line down and I can get up!"

The corporal completely ignored Mad Dog's orders and went on down to help his sergeant. When he got there, Mad Dog tried to sit up. The corporal helped, as Mad Dog very obviously was in a lot of pain.

He sat Mad Dog up and said, "Let me get this rope around you."

Mad Dog said, "No, I think some ribs are broken. We're going to have to do it another way. I'll try to climb up. You climb up behind me, but keep the rope tight."

The corporal yelled up to Rofsky. "Keep this line tight! I can't secure Mad Dog to it. I think he has some busted ribs. He's going to use the rope to climb up and I'll be behind him in case he falls."

The men all understood what this meant and quickly tightened the rope. Mad Dog painstakingly started to work his way up. In the meantime the radio operator radioed for rescue choppers to come in and remove the wounded and the dead.

Mad Dog would make a few inches and have to rest. He was perspiring heavily and uncontrollably. Slowly he inched his way up. A few times he fell against his corporal, who steadied him until he could painfully begin to move on. Finally, after painfully dragging himself up the rope an inch at a time, Mad Dog made the last few excruciating feet to the top. The waiting corpsman moved to him quickly and examined him.

"You're right, Dog. You do have some broken ribs. Your arms and shoulders are bruised up pretty good too, but I don't think anything else is broken."

The radio crackled to life. They were told to be prepared to be evacuated; the choppers were on their way. The men moved to gather their gear. Suddenly Gunny Arno appeared and was ready to be in charge again. The men were all gathered closely, but they were careful to get between rocks so that if the mortars began again they would be protected. Arno started giving orders. The men were too disgusted and stupefied even to respond.

No one had to give Mad Dog's well-trained men orders. When the choppers came they quickly got the most seriously wounded aboard. And when the next ones came in they loaded the bodies. They knew that even though Mad Dog was wounded he would be the last one out.

Gunny Arno had been among the first to board the first chopper with the wounded. Incredibly, he was the only one who didn't get some sort of wound, be it rocks or shrapnel, from the mortars.

When they got back to Dong Ha, the captain and Oop were waiting for the men, along with the colonel who was in charge of Rofsky's group. Arno, who had gotten there perhaps fifteen minutes before Mad Dog, was giving a report making it sound like it was the most harrowing experience in his life, and that he was

some sort of hero. Everyone listened calmly. They were all waiting for Mad Dog to report his views on what had happened.

They tried to get Mad Dog to stretch out on a litter so they
could carry him. He refused. He got off the chopper in obvious
pain. The captain and Oop were waiting with a jeep to take him
to the hospital.

Mad Dog said, "Have everybody checked out. I think everybody got hit one way or the other."

"Dog, we have to take care of you first. You're the most seriously injured," the captain answered.

Mad Dog looked at the captain. "Captain, please take care of
my men."

The men were promptly whisked over to the field hospital
with Mad Dog riding in the front of the jeep, the captain driving,
and Oop and the captain's shotgun on the rear seat.

Mad Dog was in a lot of pain. The x-rays revealed several
cracked ribs. There were also some nasty scrapes and deep cuts,
but because of his great physical condition, all this, in his mind,
was minor. He took Oop aside, and in private told him about
Arno ducking when one of the men was exposed.

His voice calm but icy, he finished by adding, "I don't want to
say anything, Oop, because everybody knows I don't like him or
get along with him. But if they ever send that son of a bitch, billy-
goat-smelling asshole out in the field with me again, he won't
come back!"

Oop, being the salty veteran that he was, knew that this wasn't
the time to try to reason with Mad Dog.

"Take it easy and don't get excited now, Dog. Let's get you
taken care of," he replied and turned to the waiting medics.

Mad Dog was taken care of and was told he would be staying in the field hospital a few days. Mad Dog approached the
doctor.

"Look, doc," he said, "we're camped less than a mile from
here. Can't I just go over there and stay?"

The doctor, who had treated Mad Dog before, knew the type
of individual he was.

"Yeah, go ahead. But you'll have to come in every day and get
this checked out before you can get back to combat."

Mad Dog agreed and went outside. Oop now was the only one there other than the ones who had to stay.

"Oop, I'm going to see each guy; then I'll be right out."

"Okay, I'll go with you."

They visited the men who had to stay. Mad Dog told them, "I'll be in to see you guys every day."

He went out and got into the jeep that Oop was now driving, the captain having gotten another way back to the area. They drove on, ignoring the beautiful sunset that was glowing over the not-too-distant South China Sea.

RATS

Mad Dog was true to his word. He visited his men each day, walking to the field hospital. Normally the men wouldn't have stayed at that hospital. The more seriously injured were transferred to hospital ships, but these wounds were not considered life-threatening and there was not a lot of action, so the men stayed close by their unit.

Several of the men decided to poke around the village. They returned several hours later, having bought different junk items. Some bought chickens to try to have a decent meal. Others bought rice or the rank Bami Ba beer, trading C rations for these items. When they got the bottles of beer into the tent, Mad Dog picked up a bottle and held it to the sunlight.

"Holy shit, man, this stuff is full of crap! There's scum floating in this unopened bottle!"

Several of the men who had drunk it got dysentery so badly that they couldn't even wear trousers or underwear. They were in a continual state of undress walking back and forth to the head, but they soon had no control over themselves, and had to be checked in to the field hospital. The rice had also been deliberately tainted and, of course, the men who had eaten it also got dysentery. Between this and malaria, most of the men in the company were out of action.

It's odd that a lot of people are afraid of snakes. Vietnam is full of snakes . . . everything from cobras to kraits to harmless rat snakes and everything in between. But the one thing that scared the men the most was rats. Everywhere the Marines or the Army or the Air Force set up camp, the rats followed. The American troops were good providers.

Most of the men in Mad Dog's platoon were edgy because of the combat and the constant state of alert that they were in.

One night about two in the morning, a rat jumped on one of the men's beds and somehow got under his mosquito netting. The man started screaming and jumped up and ran out with his mosquito netting still attached to him, leaving the rat in the dust and running for cover.

It was a most terrifying incident for all of the men. When it began, some of the men were in peaceful sleep, and some in fitful sleep. When the man leaped up so suddenly, shrieking, screaming, and running out of the place in total terror, all of the men jumped up and grabbed their weapons around the deck trying to figure out what was going on and looking for the attackers.

When they finally caught the young Marine and wrestled him to the ground, all he could say was, "Rats! Rats! Rats!" over and over again. They finally got him calmed down. The next day he was sent out of combat to headquarters duty in Da Nang.

A DULL DAY
AT THE COMPOUND

The Marines in Dong Ha had locals do their laundry, make their beds—what there was to make—and air out their sleeping bags. Some had bought crude futon mattresses to put on their cots. They were a real luxury.

Mad Dog was almost completely healed. One day, Oop stopped by to see him.

"Want to go with me to Hue? We're moving a convoy of trucks and equipment."

"Sure, why not," replied Mad Dog, who was ready to do anything to relieve the tension and boredom. He grabbed his rifle and web belt with his canteens on, went out, and got into the jeep.

When Oop turned on the ignition, a stream of sparks like a sparkler started shooting down under the dash on to his legs. Without saying a word, they both bailed out of the jeep and rolled away in opposite directions. The sparks continued. Mad Dog ran around the jeep to the driver's side, reached up under the dash, and pulled some wires loose. The sparks stopped.

"What in the hell was that?"

"I dunno. We better take a look," Oop said as he bent under the dash.

"Shit!!! It's a fuckin' grenade!!! The weight of it must have shorted these wires and caused the sparking. Look at that! The damned thing's a dud!"

They got a motor pool sergeant to come over and look at the jeep. He made quick repairs and they were off on their drive to Hue. As they pulled out of the camp, Mad Dog turned to Oop.

"It sure is boring as hell around here," he said. "Let's go see if we can find some action elsewhere. I think we've worn out our welcome here!"

Oop laughed. "Yeah. Let's see what happens with these big guys."

He pulled into the middle of a line of six-by's that were picking up speed. It was exciting to see the big six-by's (two-and-a-half-ton trucks) and the little jeep as they flew, literally flew, down the highway. The two men whooped it up as they tore on down the road.

Mad Dog and Oop went into Hue, which at the time was fairly secure, and visited some old friends of theirs. Then they headed to the super secret compound where Sergeant Rofsky was headquartered. They pulled up to the gate and stopped to talk to the sentry.

"We're friends of Sergeant Rofsky. We were together at the rock pile and thought we'd stop by to see how he's doin'. Would you let him know we're here? My name's Oop and this here is Mad Dog."

"Yeah, sure, I'll call him. Wait here."

In a few moments, Sergeant Rofsky appeared at the gate.

"Man, it's good to see you," he grinned. "Glad you're up and at it, Mad Dog. I'm really sorry, you guys, but I can't let you in right now. We're up to our ears in it. I'll have to catch ya later."

"Yeah, that's okay, Sarge. We're on our way back. We just came by to say hi. We drove down here to ease the boredom."

"Well, I'll catch up to you guys soon," Rofsky replied.

"That's great! We'll see ya."

"Take it easy, buddy," Mad Dog called as they waved their good-byes and headed back to join their convoy.

MONTAGNARD

The next morning, Captain Raye's company moved out for a search and destroy patrol. He had been ordered to stop at a Montagnard village and ask the head man for guides. Captain Raye called Oop in to discuss this with him.

"Oop, we're going to a Montagnard village. I've been ordered to ask them for guides for our S and D patrol. Got any suggestions?"

"You should find out who the head man is, and go to him. You got to get his blessing if we're going to get anywhere. Give the gifts to him, not to the kids. Giving gifts to kids insults the elders and they'll lose face. You gotta be careful that doesn't happen. These Orientals are touchy when it comes to losing face."

When they arrived at the village, Captain Raye had the interpreter speak to the head man as best he could, using the Montagnard language. Captain Raye presented gifts to the head man. Each gift was appreciated: cigars, cigarettes, matches, chocolate . . . until the soap.

The head man bit into it. He sat there with a pained look on his face.

Oop, with quick thinking, hurriedly told the interpreter to say to the head man in a loud voice, "You are very wise to check the quality of soap that way! But we always check it before we give it to someone as honorable as the chief."

The head man puffed up his chest and nodded approval. This was a great face-saver, and the head man was instantly loyal to the Marines. Captain Raye turned to the interpreter.

"Ask the head man if he would permit his corpsmen to show the women how to use the soap on the children."

Many of the children had sores and rashes. The head man nodded his permission. The corpsmen and Marines bathed the children very gently and carefully. The Marines had made inroads with the entire village by this time.

When the bathing of the children was completed, the head man offered women to the captain and Oop to relieve their tension. Although it was a great insult under normal circumstances to refuse a gift from the head man, Oop had the interpreter tell the chief that they looked forward to using the women when they returned from their patrol, but that now they had to move on to do their duty.

The head man gave the company three guides to lead them to their objectives. After a week of small insignificant contacts the company was ordered back to Cam Lo. As the Marines were heading back to the Montagnard village with the guides, the point man stopped.

"I'm smelling a horrible stench in the air," he said. "I wonder what the hell it is."

Soon everyone could smell it. The men began gagging, some covered up their faces with handkerchiefs, while others gutted it out. They rounded a turn and the Montagnard village came into view. The source of the stench was clear.

The Montagnard village had been burnt to the ground. All the inhabitants were burnt to a crisp. The North Vietnamese had ringed the village with flame throwers and burnt the buildings and all the occupants of the village alive.

Some of the Marines walked with the guides, turning over bodies. There were mothers, still clutching their babies to their breasts, and the children the Marines had washed so gently only days before. All were burnt black beyond recognition.

Captain Raye radioed headquarters.

"This is Captain Raye. We're here at the Montagnard village. It's been burnt to the ground and all the villagers were blasted with flame throwers. Requesting equipment to bury the bodies. The entire village, except for the three guides, are dead. Those motherfuckers fried them all!"

The sight and odor stayed in the mind's eye of many of the men for a long time.

BLOOD BATH

On return to Cam Lo the company was assigned perimeter guard around the main encampment. This was to give the men some rest, a bath, a hot meal, and a cold drink. Not having ice is something most people can't really fathom. Days of 120°-plus temperatures leaves only warm water to drink, yet somehow the C-rations seemed cold. Most of the men hadn't seen ice since they had landed in Vietnam. Several of the men got cramps from drinking the cold drinks too fast.

Oop's sector of the perimeter was on a slight hill in the middle of a very wide, flat valley. At 0300 in the morning, the men on duty noted movement. They called Mad Dog, who was in charge at the time. He listened and popped a flare. The valley seemed to be full of N.V.A. regulars led by sappers with explosives strapped to their bodies. These explosive-laden human kamikazes tried to jump on equipment or groups of men to explode themselves and everything else in range. Mad Dog immediately called headquarters.

"This is Boxer 44. Our entire sector is under attack by at least a battalion of N.V.A. regulars. Give us some flares and H.E. (high explosives)."

The voice at the other end of the radio said, "Roger, how many of them . . ."

The Dog cut him off.

"We ain't got time to socialize! The little bastards are here!"

The sound of the weapons convinced whoever it was on the other end of the radio to shut up and get busy.

The sappers came in first.

The Marines went into hand-to-hand combat using bayonets, knives, machetes, entrenching tools . . . anything deadly that they could grab. Some of the men, aiming as carefully as they could, began to shoot the sappers through the head—this so that they wouldn't hit the explosives around their middles and blow up the sapper and their own buddies along with them.

Others fought a deadly hand-to-hand battle to protect their buddies and equipment. The sappers were annihilated in front of Mad Dog's position, but there was no time to rest. The N.V.A.s came flooding in.

Mad Dog set off claymore mines that went ripping through the ranks of the N.V.A. Some of them were running in such a frenzied state that the claymores ripped one or both feet off—yet they continued their fanatical charge on stumps until their brains realized they were dead or dying and they dropped over.

Oop ran to help Mad Dog's position and jumped to a twin-mounted 50-calibre machine gun that had been set up for anti-aircraft use. The bullets had explosive heads so that they exploded on impact.

Oop yelled to one of the troops running with him, "You feed. I'll fire!"

Oop opened fire, going back and forth across the valley chopping the N.V.A.s to ribbons. One of the N.V.A.s was cut in two by the exploding bullets. His torso hung in the air for what seemed an eternity, but in truth was probably a tenth of a second, while his legs did a crazy bowlegged trot before falling over at least ten feet from the body.

One of the N.V.A.s who had been shot in the stomach staggered forward. He ran his bayonet through Mad Dog's boot, falling dead on it, pinning Mad Dog to the ground. One of the Marines saw that Mad Dog couldn't move and yelled, "Corpsman! Corpsman! Help Mad Dog! Let's go, Marines! They got Mad Dog!"

The P.F.C. led the Marines' charge down the hill to protect his sergeant. The corpsman ran to Mad Dog and began violently jerking the body of the dead N.V.A. soldier away from the impaled Marine. Mad Dog pulled the bayonet out of his foot.

The N.V.A.s were now fleeing to the right, heading for the nearest side of the valley. Just then the drone of "Puff the Magic Dragon" was heard, and she dropped a flare. It lit up almost the entire valley. The pilot needed no instructions from the ground. He banked Puff to deliver her deadly cargo. At night this was a most spectacular sight. It looked as though streams of flames belched out of her side delivering the fire from her mini-guns on the fleeing Vietnamese.

The next morning, North Vietnamese bodies were in grotesque positions, torn apart by claymores, the twin fifties, and Puff. Some of the dead faces were people they recognized. They had been working in the camp. The Vietnamese man the camp had used as a barber was found dead in an N.V.A. captain's uniform, and the woman in pink lay dead in the uniform of an N.V.A. lieutenant.

Captain Raye had been seriously wounded and was being medevacuated. He requested to see his officers Oop and Mad Dog before he was flown away. In a weak voice he whispered, "Take care of yourselves and my Marines. I'll be back!" He was then whisked away aboard a chopper.

There were many wounded that day. Mad Dog waited until last to have the corpsman look at him. When the corpsman took a look at Mad Dog's foot, he shook his head as he looked up.

"Dog, I can't do this for you. I'm totally out of sterile sutures. You'll have to go to the field hospital and have this taken care of."

"Aw, com'on, man! It ain't that bad! Just sew it up with regular thread. I'll get my sewing kit. You can use that thread."

"This wound's pretty bad. I don't think you should do this."

"I don't want to take the time to go to the hospital. It'll be fine."

"Okay. You're the boss!"

The corpsman stitched up the wound, but in a few days the foot was hopelessly infected. This time Mad Dog had to go to the field hospital. The doctor took a look at the swollen and angry wound between Dog's small and fourth toe, and shook his head.

"Dog," he said, "this is going to hurt you a lot more than me!"

He poured disinfectant on the foot and tore the toes apart. Pus flew in all directions as Mad Dog's head jerked back. The doctor cut out the thread and thoroughly bathed the wound.

"You dumb shit," he exclaimed. "If you had had this taken care of in the first place, this wouldn't have happened! You aren't good to anybody when you're laid up with an infection! When you're wounded, you come here and have it taken care of. Then when we need you, you'll be able to do something about it. Now you're going to have to be here until this mess heals properly."

Mad Dog almost agreed with him. He was kept in the hospital for three days until the infection was arrested, then for another week, he had to wear a shower sandal on the damaged foot.

TRAPPED

Two weeks went by and Mad Dog's wound was pretty well healed. The company had a new commanding officer; his name was Zalor. He was a good intelligence officer, but he had never commanded troops in combat.

He called all of the officers first, and then the N.C.O.s to tell them that he was the new C.O. and to get to know them a little. He told them that the company would be setting up a night ambush. He ordered that each N.C.O. check his men to be sure everyone was prepared properly. This was unnecessary but Zalor had no way yet of knowing his men or their capabilities. He asked Oop to stay after the meeting.

"Gunny Clarke," Zalor began, "I understand you are very experienced in the field. What, if any, advice would you offer concerning the upcoming duty?"

"Captain, I recommend that you try to stay close to Mad Dog or myself if we get in any kind of trouble. I completely trust Mad Dog and you can rely on his judgment. Unfortunately he acts on instincts and doesn't talk much."

"Thank you, Gunny. That will be all."

Captain Zalor introduced himself to each member of the company to get a "feel" for his men. They moved out shortly after he completed his rounds. The choppers were waiting and took off as soon as the men were aboard.

Once there, the Marines unloaded and quickly moved to the ambush positions. Shortly after dark fell, movement was detected and noises were heard in the company ambush sight. An overeager Marine opened fire.

Unknown to the Marines, the N.V.A. had set a trap for them. The company had spotted them during the chopper drop-off and the N.V.A. moved troops in hoping to annihilate the Marines. The N.V.A. hit hard and fast, outnumbering the Marines three to one. Some of the Marines were separated by the flood of troops moving through the openings the N.V.A. made in the Marine lines. Many of the others managed to hold their positions, somehow keeping teams and squads together. Exploding hand grenades, hand-to-hand combat, and intense firefights raged for two eternities.

In the morning the Marines started to communicate verbally with each other. They radioed headquarters for reinforcements and to remove their dead and wounded. All of the company officers had been wounded. Captain Zalor and three men were missing. Oop set up patrols to move the wounded and dead to the edge of the clearing where the choppers would land to remove them. Mad Dog was sent on a patrol to look for the missing captain and men.

He found Captain Zalor. His head was mounted on a stake. His penis was in his mouth. His body was not to be found. Mad Dog went livid with rage.

"Those godless motherfucking yellow sons of bitches gooks. They'll pay for this!"

He searched again for the body, and for signs of the other missing men. Finally, unable to find any signs of blood or drag marks, he removed the captain's head from the stake and gently wrapped it in his poncho. His face still black with rage and hate, he headed back to the landing zone.

The choppers with the relief troops were arriving as Mad Dog got to the clearing with his grisly cargo in hand. In the confusion of the previous night the Marines had captured three N.V.A.s. Oop, seeing Mad Dog and realizing what he was carrying by the look on Mad Dog's face, turned to four of his men and spoke quietly.

"Hold those three in the jungle. Don't report this to anyone. Just do it!"

No more needed to be said. Oop knew his men were extremely loyal.

Oop kept the interpreter, Mad Dog and the four Marines who were guarding the prisoners with him. He deliberately lagged behind so that they could board the last chopper. Then, addressing the pilot, Oop said, "Take it straight up. I want those N.V.A. bastards to see us."

He turned to the interpreter and pointed to one of the N.V.A.s who was particularly obstinate. "Ask him who his commanding officer is."

The North Vietnamese, sneering, replied, "Vietnamese tough. Vietnamese strong. Vietnamese not afraid."

Mad Dog, with the memory of Captain Zalor still burning in his mind, jumped up and kicked him out the door of the chopper.

Mad Dog stood and looked at him falling to his death. "Vietnamese can't fly," he snarled through gritted teeth. "Rot in hell you little yellow motherfucker."

One of the other prisoners wet his pants and started chattering and clucking.

"Ask him who his commanding officer is," Oop grunted.

Pointing at Mad Dog with the fear of God in their eyes, the remaining two prisoners spoke almost in unison.

"He just kicked him out!"

Oop sat down. He knew that these two would be more accommodating about giving information when they were interrogated at headquarters.

Immediately upon arriving at headquarters Oop approached the colonel.

"Colonel Nordstrom, I'm requesting your permission to mount a rescue patrol for the missing Marines. The sooner we move to rescue our men the better chance we have of getting them back."

Colonel Nordstrom answered, "Get your patrol and get back out there. I'll radio the company that's in place that you'll be coming back."

The six Marines reboarded the chopper and it rushed them back to where it had picked them up a few minutes before. Oop led the recon patrol through the jungle following whatever signs they could find . . . blood spots, drag marks, etc.

They came upon an N.V.A. soldier heeding the call of nature. He never rose from his squatted position. Mad Dog made short neat work of him with his K-bar and hid his body further back into the jungle. The Marine patrol knew they were close and became more cautious and slow-moving than before.

Oop spotted a cage in the clearing. It held the three missing Marines. There was only one guard. The N.V.A. obviously felt if the Americans tried a rescue it would be at night. The closest jungle cover to the cage was to the right of Oop and his men. Oop radioed the company commander and gave their position.

"When you hear us open fire start moving on the double," he cautioned. "Mad Dog, you get those guys out of there. Men, spread out and we'll cover them."

Mad Dog and his two men worked their way around to the closest point in the jungle to the cage. As Mad Dog moved slowly into position he saw that two of the captured Marines were shoeless and seemed to be nursing their hands. The third, a black Marine, was fully clothed and apparently unhurt. Mad Dog crept to the back of the bamboo cage while his two men covered him. If he needed help to move the prisoners he would signal.

The N.V.A. guard seemingly was tired and turned only occasionally to look at the prisoners while he sat with his back against the cage. Mad Dog got to the rear of the cage without being seen and pressed himself against it to take advantage of the shadows to camouflage himself. He saw that all of the prisoners could move. He also saw that the N.V.A. had pulled the fingernails off the two white Marines, trying to turn the black Marine against them.

Mad Dog slipped his K-bar through the bars of the cage. The black Marine took it just as the N.V.A. guard was turning to check the prisoners.

Thinking quickly, one of the captured men moved to the side of the cage and started urinating. The guard chuckled and turned again with his back to the cage.

Activity in the camp was nil. Flies buzzed and birds let out a squawk in the jungle now and then. Every minute seemed to freeze into hours. Occasionally one of the N.V.A. would make a head call in the jungle.

Mad Dog offered his bayonet to the prisoner closest to him and motioned to cut the ropes holding the cage door shut. As soon as his buddy had gotten a hold on the bayonet, Carl, the black Marine, moved quickly and with deadly skill. He reached through the bars and clamped one hand over the N.V.A.'s mouth and jammed the K-bar into his back. It wasn't a clean kill. Carl twisted the K-bar and rammed it in harder. The struggling stopped.

Another eternity passed.

The Marine with the bayonet, sweat pouring from his face with the pain of grasping the bayonet with his torn fingers, cut the bottom rope holding the cage door. Carl made short work of the other two. The three were out quickly and softly closed the door.

Just as they reached the jungle they were spotted by an N.V.A. leaving his tent. Oop's men and the two men covering Mad Dog opened fire, throwing grenades and firing their grenade launcher. The relief company heard the shots and started running to rescue their buddies. Mad Dog and Oop held their positions until the Marines coming to rescue them overran the N.V.A. camp. Mad Dog called for stretchers to remove the two Marines who had no boots.

They were quickly helped on to stretchers, but as the men picked up the stretchers and began to run with them, three N.V.A.s came running at them from their left side. Mad Dog cut them down in their tracks. Then he spotted a fuel tank, and threw two grenades. The fuel exploded and a spectacular fire erupted and sent smoke billowing thousands of feet into the sky.

Mad Dog turned. An N.V.A. was poised to decapitate him with a machete. Mad Dog's rifle was on automatic. He fired point-blank into the N.V.A.'s face and neck. The commie's head all but disappeared in a sea of red.

Mad Dog was now moving full speed through the jungle. A few N.V.A.s continued to pop up at varying intervals. Mad Dog was in his element—firing his rifle, throwing grenades and screaming like a raving maniac. He caught Oop at the clearing. The choppers were waiting. Mad Dog, never breaking stride, leaped onto the chopper as it was lifting off.

ENLISTED MEN'S
JUSTICE

When they got back to the C.P. they were told that the company would be getting some in-country rest and that some men would be going on R and R.

Mad Dog had never reported any of the wounds he had received because if a man was wounded twice he would be sent out of Vietnam. Mad Dog certainly didn't want that. In the rescue he had gotten a nasty gash in his leg and had to have it tended to. He still refused to let anyone call it a war wound and told the doctors and corpsmen not to classify it as such. They couldn't believe their ears. They were far more familiar with guys insisting that some very shaky wounds were purple heart material, and here was a man insisting his wasn't.

The doctor told Mad Dog that he had to report every day to have the dressings changed. He also wisely told him that he would be back in combat faster if he kept the wounds attended to. The doctor felt this was the only way to get Mad Dog to come for a dressing change regularly.

Meanwhile, there at headquarters, the famous shit hole incident took place. A male Red Cross worker would walk to the crapper every morning, sit down, light a cigarette, and read the latest edition of *The Stars and Stripes*.

You had to see the crappers to believe them. This one was built over a pit for this purpose: each morning the crapper building was tilted and laid on its back. Diesel fuel was poured on the crap in the pit and set on fire.

One morning, Mad Dog saw the Red Cross person with the paper.

"Hey, buddy," he said, "how about letting me read your paper when you're done."

From the reaction of the man, you would have thought that Mad Dog had asked to screw his wife. He began to lecture. "I," he grandly stated, "am equal in rank to a full colonel." He barked at Mad Dog, "Who do you think you are approaching me so casually?"

Mad Dog's expression never changed. "I thought I had asked a man for a newspaper, but I see now I was wrong," he spoke calmly.

The man started a faint smile.

"I see I asked an asshole," Mad Dog finished.

The asshole was so flabbergasted that he started flapping his arms and muttering.

"I hold rank around here. You don't know who you're talking to like that," etc., etc. The few men who were in the vicinity thought he was attempting a take off.

Three shit commandos (the guys in charge of burning the crap) happened to hear what had happened and stopped Mad Dog.

"Be here tomorrow morning," they told Mad Dog. "We've got something in mind for this king of the shit house."

The next morning Mad Dog noticed that a lot of Marines were in the area pretending to be busy, but were in fact just screwing around. The king, right on schedule, was strutting to his throne. A few of the Marines threw him a salute and he saluted back. He was all smiles.

One of the shit commandos, grinning from ear to ear, spoke.

"Watch this. We poured straight gasoline in the shit and didn't burn it."

The shit house king sat down, lit his cigarette, and threw the match down the hole beside him. Flames shot up through the three unoccupied holes. The man's ass and balls took the brunt of what tried to escape from the hole he was sitting on. He screamed in surprise and pain.

He came out of the crapper, pants down, legs apart, and for some reason, bent over at the waist. He waddled this way to the field hospital as the shit house went up in flames in roaring tribute to the ingenuity of Marine Corps enlisted men.

When word got around headquarters of what happened, several staff N.C.O.s and officers tried to figure a way to give the shit commandos a medal.

However, protocol called for them to be warned to be more careful, and a lieutenant called them together, officially telling them to be more careful.

The lance corporal in charge said, "Yeah, guys. If we fuck up again they'll take us off shit patrol and kick us out of Vietnam!"

The lieutenant fought to control himself but broke into gales of laughter when he tried to retell the story to the other officers. Everyone had a wild howling laugh about it, except of course, for Lieutenant Fenig.

ROADSIDE STAND

Captain Wilson was called to a meeting. The colonel in charge notified him that his company would be providing security for an artillery battery. He started to protest but the colonel stopped him, saying it was temporary, and gave him orders to proceed. Captain Wilson prepared the troops and they left. They traveled by truck and jeep to the site, where they were to set up a defensive perimeter, and wait for the artillery to arrive.

Oop and Captain Wilson were traveling in the same jeep. The captain had been given air photos of the area, and was looking them over again. As they were approaching, he noticed what appeared to be two large buildings near the side of the road that were not in the photograph. When they arrived at the site, the "buildings" were in fact two stacks—one of beer and the other of Coke.

A gleeful Vietnamese was by the roadside calling, "I sell beer cheap." The captain looked at Oop almost in shock wondering, "How the hell did this asshole know we were coming?"

Oop got out of the jeep and directed the men to load the pop and beer on an empty trailer behind one of the trucks and to put the rest on the truck.

The Vietnamese was happily clucking and trying to negotiate a job with the captain, who had no idea what Oop, meanwhile, was up to. When the men had loaded all the beer and soda, the V.N. said, "You pay me eight hundred American dollars."

Oop, coming up to him from behind the jeep, said, "Where's the factory in Vietnam?"

The V.N. looked confused and did not answer.

Oop added, "You stole my beer."

The V.N., visibly excited, said, "You pay! You pay!"

Oop drew his pistol, cocked it, grabbed the V.N. by the head and ran the barrel into his mouth.

He calmly said, "You stole my beer, asshole."

The Marines were frozen. They weren't sure what Oop was going to do. The V.N. was not so cocksure as he had been, but in fact seemed ready to have a heart attack.

Oop smiled and said again very calmly, "You stole my beer. I don't like people stealing my beer. I'm going to blow your fucking brains all over this shithole you call Vietnam."

The V.N. sank to his knees in terror. Oop took the .45 out of his mouth and turned to the captain.

"This guy is an N.V.A. agent. Better get a chopper to take him back. Also tell the colonel that there are some N.V.A. agents in camp. That's who tipped them off that we were coming."

The captain immediately got headquarters on the radio and told the colonel what had happened and what Oop had suggested. The colonel took swift action and discovered ten N.V.A.s working in the camp in various jobs.

SUPER SECRET

The artillery battery arrived and set up the next day. As happened everywhere in Vietnam, miles away from any villages, Vietnamese began to show up looking for work. Chatter in pidgin English could be heard.

"Me number one barber," or "Me do number one laundry."

Although Captain Wilson was in charge of protecting the artillery battery, Lieutenant Colonel Carrington of the artillery battery was in overall charge, and made no bones about having his influence felt. Captain Wilson spoke to the lieutenant colonel.

"Sir, I feel that we should keep the Vietnamese nationals away from our camp. We've had trouble in the past and this is a good way to avoid it."

The colonel, ignoring Captain Wilson's advice, replied, "These people can make life easier around here." He then added, "Is there anything else, Captain?"

Captain Wilson replied, "No, sir."

The colonel said, "That will be all."

As Captain Wilson turned to leave the colonel added, "One more thing, Captain. I want you to remove all of the concertina wire to the east."

Captain Wilson, shocked, protested, "But Colonel . . ."

He was cut off by the colonel saying, "I'm very busy, Captain. Just do it."

Captain Wilson didn't reply. He turned and left.

The concertina wire was removed as ordered. The artillery commander never did explain his reasoning for this most insane order.

Early that afternoon the general arrived on a helicopter to check the artillery battery. He spoke to the battery commander first and then asked for a tour of the defenses. When the general spoke to Captain Wilson his first question was, "Why is there no concertina across the valley which is the most accessible approach to the guns?"

Captain Wilson calmly stated, "Colonel Carrington ordered me to have it removed."

Carrington gulped and said, "It was only temporary to move the guns around."

The general looked at him in amazement while questioning in his own mind what exactly was Carrington's reasoning. The general came to the silent conclusion that Carrington wanted to command infantry troops and his judgment was clouded by the thrill of the moment.

Carrington turned to Captain Wilson, "Captain, have your men install the wire immediately."

"Yes, sir," Captain Wilson acknowledged.

Darkness would fall before any major headway could be made in reinstalling the protective wire. The general informed Carrington, his executive officer Major Garcia, and Captain Wilson that intelligence reports indicated a company-sized N.V.A. unit to the direct east of the artillery position. A four-man team of electronic intelligence gatherers had arrived with the general on his gunship headed by Mad Dog's old friend, Rofsky.

The general said, "The information that these Marines give you has been proven to be very credible and should be considered strongly in any tactical situation."

The sergeant in charge of the intelligence team, Sergeant Rofsky, reported to the officer. "General, all of our equipment is set up and operational."

The general introduced the three officers to Sergeant Rofsky and asked the colonel to have the first sergeant join them to meet the super secret Marine. The general knew that Sergeant Rofsky would get more done through the first sergeant than through the battery commander. The general and his aides boarded their choppers and left.

Dark had fallen when Sergeant Rofsky intercepted some enemy radio transmissions. He went to the C.P. and approached the first sergeant.

"First Sergeant, we have several quick transmissions to the N.V.A. unit in our vicinity. My men and I think that an attack is imminent."

The first sergeant sent for Captain Wilson, Colonel Carrington and Major Garcia. Garcia entered the C.P. as the runner was leaving. The first sergeant had Sergeant Rofsky fill them in on what he suspected. Major Garcia ordered half of the big guns turned to the east, filled with buckshot and lowered to minimum heights.

After Wilson was informed he personally went to each platoon commander and ordered them to be on full alert and to have all their men in position. Wilson felt there were N.V.A. agents in the camp during the day, so he quickly reset the machine gun positions, and ordered Oop to booby-trap the abandoned position and reset some of the claymore mines.

His suspicions were justified. As soon as the attack began, N.V.A. crept to the abandoned bunker hoping to eliminate the machine gun nest. When they stormed it, the trip wire inside the bunker was released and blew the bunker and the N.V.A. to bits.

The main N.V.A. force then started its attack. The Marines shot flares into the night sky to see the N.V.A. running to the artillery battery in controlled groups of three, four, or five men or women. The repositioned machine guns were herding the N.V.A. into the deadly trough of the artillery buckshot.

When the attack started, Lieutenant Colonel Carrington and a gunnery sergeant, for reasons known only to them and God, ran into a tent. An N.V.A. machine gunner raked the tent over and over, riddling both men with bullets, killing them almost instantly.

Major Garcia had told the gun crews to hold their fire until they would have maximum effect. The untested Marines responded perfectly, waiting while the infantry company herded the N.V.A. into the range of the deadly big guns. The artillery opened fire with devastating effect, mowing down the attackers with such deadly force and accuracy that it was almost over after one barrage. Brief hand-to-hand combat took place in several areas with the Marines subduing the N.V.A. quickly and capturing the wounded N.V.A.s.

No one slept that night. The experienced men knew the attack was over but spent the night calming the newer men's jittery nerves. The morning sun exposed the mayhem brought by the artillery. A gruesome scene with bodies, parts of bodies, and some unrecognizable masses that would have been difficult to ever associate with having been human at one time spread out before the eye.

The general arrived just after first light and toured the area. He congratulated Major Garcia, Captain Wilson and Sergeant Rofsky. The Marines had mauled the N.V.A., killing one hundred and twenty-four and capturing six. They suspected that a few may have escaped. The N.V.A. prisoners were taken away under guard to be questioned by interpreters. The dead bodies were searched for military documents and then buried in a mass grave.

The Marines suffered two dead and eight wounded. The wounded Marines were whisked away by helicopter. The general asked Sergeant Rofsky if there had been enemy radio activity in the area.

Sergeant Rofsky replied, "General, there were a lot of transmissions coming from the area of that mountain." He looked toward the northwest and pointed it out. He said, "If you come to where our directions finders are set up, I'll give you the coordinates on the map."

The general said, "I'll meet you there in a few minutes."

Sergeant Rofsky excused himself and returned to his position.

The general told Major Garcia to stand by to put fifty high explosive rounds and fifty white phosphorus rounds on the coor-

dinates that he would come back with. Major Garcia acknowledged the order, and excused himself to have the guns turned
around and zeroed in on the mountain. He knew which mountain
Sergeant Rofsky was speaking of, as he was there when the
sergeant pointed. All he needed was to get bearings and distance. Then he left to prepare his artillery battery in prepara-
tion for the final coordinates.

The general went to Sergeant Rofsky's position. Sergeant
Rofsky was very brief, pointing out the area and giving the coordinates. The general said, "Well done. If this is the only activity,
pack up and get on my gun ship. I want you to take care of something else for me."

Rofsky said, "Yes, sir," as the general walked away toward
Major Garcia's command post. Sergeant Rofsky ordered his men
to tear down their equipment.

As soon as he was given the coordinates, Major Garcia gave
the orders and the big guns opened up. The explosions from the
artillery ripped the mountainside, setting off a multitude of sec-
ondary explosions that sent smoke billowing thousands of feet
into the air.

Without having further reconnaissance, the general knew
that this had been a major staging area for the North
Vietnamese with supplies, ammunition, and gasoline.

After the barrage was over, Major Garcia walked the general
to where Sergeant Rofsky's men had their disassembled equipment ready to load on the general's gunship. Again the general
congratulated Sergeant Rofsky and his men and told them to get
aboard. The men boarded the chopper, the general boarded his,
and they were off for a new assignment.

THE HAWK

Oop had some old Marine buddies who were with a Hawk Missile detachment stationed on Marble Mountain, just outside of Da Nang. He scrounged a jeep and asked Mad Dog if he wanted to take a ride to meet some of his pals. Mad Dog agreed and off they went to the top of the hill.

Oop found his friends and they showed him and Mad Dog around explaining the different functions of the Missile Men. There had been some reports of N.V. MIGs and helicopters but none actually sighted this far south. The men in the missile company were anxious to show their skills and knock down an enemy aircraft. The opportunity had not presented itself, and of course this was frustrating to all.

As Oop and Mad Dog were walking to their jeep the men invited them back when they could spend the night and hoist a few brews. Just then a young Marine burst out of the trailer that housed the radar and fire control for the missiles and said, "Top, we got contact with a Bogey."

The top (master sergeant) took off at a gallop to the trailer with everyone but Oop and Mad Dog following. They got in the jeep and started down the winding dirt road back to Da Nang.

The Hawk missilemen did their job beautifully, calculations, etc., etc., and fired the missile. It rose perhaps 200 feet and then started to pinwheel end over end like a giant fireworks display. The destruct mechanism was employed and the missile exploded and rained fire and debris over the jungle and countryside.

Mad Dog quipped to Oop, "We really can train Marines, but we sure as hell can't train Hawks!"

A second missile was fired and streaked skyward. It took off in a burst of fire and noise, went up and then circled back heading straight for the jeep.

Oop was driving.

Mad Dog was watching the Hawk as it turned back toward them.

"Gunny, that Hawk just turned and headed back this way."

Oop looked up. "Oh shit!!! Bail out, Dog!"

Luckily the road was so steep that Oop was not traveling very fast. Both men jumped out and the jeep went straight over a cliff where the road curved.

The Hawk missile streaked and scored a direct hit on the jeep.

Oop and Mad Dog sat on the road looking at each other wondering what next.

Mad Dog said, "Don't fart, Gunny. I think they're heat-seekers."

The Gunny's friends at the missile site jumped in jeeps and tore down the hill at breakneck speed for the conditions to see if Oop and Mad Dog had been destroyed by the errant missile.

The lead jeep driver saw the two "devehicled" Marines and pulled to a stop far short of them and the four occupants were out and running to them. The second jeep almost rear-ended the first, but did manage to stop and its occupants went running up also.

The eight walked to the edge where the Oop's jeep had gone over the side and saw a mangled unrecognizable mess on fire and some small spots of fire around it.

No one said anything . . . or needed to. Oop said, "Can we get a jeep ride back to Da Nang?" emphasizing jeep. "I got some paper work to fill out about losing a jeep to a friendly missile."

They all laughed nervously, silently grateful that the two former occupants of the jeep were safe.

RICE PADDY RESCUE

One of Sergeant Rofsky's Super Snoop teams had disappeared and with them, their code books and radio equipment. The word spread that a volunteer was needed to deliver code books and new radios. Of course Mad Dog volunteered.

The deliveries were routine. The choppers barely landed when the Super Snoop electronic Marines were at the doors unloading the equipment and Mad Dog was handing them the code books.

The chopper pilot kept the best until last. One of the electronic recon teams was with a line company further south, close to the Ho Chi Minh Trail. They were camped in an area adjacent to some flooded rice paddies. As the chopper, about fifty feet above the ground, was coming in to land, the N.V.A. opened fire with two 50-caliber machine guns about one hundred yards apart.

The pilot was hit. The copilot grabbed the controls.

Mad Dog had bent over to pick up the last radio to hand to the waiting men when the chopper came close to landing. Just as he grabbed the last radio, the chopper tilted almost completely sideways. Mad Dog went flying out the open door of the chopper.

He twisted in the air in a slow back flip, holding the radio out to protect it. The fall seemed to take forever. Still slowly turning, he hit in a rice paddy. His legs were bent at the knee behind him and the radio slammed into his chest.

Were it not for the last code book that he had in his shirt, Mad Dog would have been knocked out by the impact of the radio and would have drowned. He was flat on his back in the mud and slimy water with the radio on his chest and his immobilized legs twisted under him. Although dazed, the natural instinct to survive kept him bobbing up to catch a few deep breaths then he would sink back down into the stinking filthy water of the rice paddy.

The Marine company was now in a full-scale fire fight, unusual for the daytime. The company commander quickly called in air support.

Sergeant Rofsky, who was in charge of the intelligence gathering team, requested permission to try to get to Mad Dog.

"Captain, I'd like to take a man and see if we can get to the Marine in the water. It looks like he's going to drown if he doesn't get help."

"Do you want one of my men or one of yours?"

"I'd like one of your men, sir, preferably a strong one. We're going to have to flip him over onto his face, then turn him on his back to pull him out."

The captain looked at his "shotgun," the Marine who for all intents and purposes was as close to a bodyguard as you can get. "Howard, do you want to volunteer?" he asked.

The corporal, hardly waiting for him to finish speaking, said, "Yes, sir!"

Rofsky spoke to Howard, briefing him on his plan.

"The surest way to Mad Dog, if there is a sure way, is directly from the point closest to him from the rice paddy dike. The biggest danger, I think, is going over the dike, since once we're in the rice paddy we'll be lower than the N.V.A. and they shouldn't be able to see us as easily once we're there."

Since the rescue would be taking place in water it would be too difficult to keep their weapons dry, so they set them aside and loaded themselves with grenades.

The decision had been made for the two Marines to go over the dike together to keep the surprise on the American side. A fire team of four Marines was sent to the dike in case the two needed help or if the N.V.A. tried to attack them while they were in the process of moving Mad Dog. The two Marines crawled to the dike and caught their breath as best they could—both of their hearts were pounding in their ears. The Marine company opened fire on the N.V.A., the two looked at each other, Rofsky nodded, and they were over the dike in one quick movement. They were almost unnoticed and proceeded to crawl in the water and slime to Mad Dog, who was growing weaker and about to accept his fate of drowning in a filthy rice paddy.

The two, Rofsky in the back, snaked their way forward to Mad Dog.

He heard them coming and faintly gasped, "Get back! I'm finished. Don't get hurt for me."

Rofsky said, "Shut up! You ain't goin' nowhere, and you got a lot more beer to drink, women to fuck and gook ass to kick!"

Mad Dog, beginning to sink again, didn't hear it all and wasn't sure who said it. Rofsky and Howard got to Mad Dog. One went to each side of him and gently lifted his head out of the water.

Rofsky said, "Get your breath, Dog. We're going to flip you over and then turn you on your back and get your ass out of here."

Mad Dog said feebly, "Okay. Do it."

The two Marines at his side reached under Mad Dog's shoulders and back and quickly flipped him over onto his face, then rolled him onto his back as the helicopter gunships and rescue chopper arrived. The gun ships came in with rockets blasting the N.V.A.'s positions. When their rocket pads were empty, on schedule F-4s came swooping in with napalm to blast the enemy positions. Rofsky and Howard were dragging Mad Dog to the dike they had come from as the medevac chopper came rushing in above them. The pilot hovered a few feet to the side and above them sending water spray to indent a water circle around them with the big blade of his aircraft. Howard picked up Mad Dog and sloshed to the chopper. Two corpsmen with a stretcher hopped off and Howard laid Mad Dog on it. They quickly got him aboard and the chopper headed for the field hospital with the most precious cargo of all—a U.S. Marine!

THE MAKING OF
MAD DOG

Mad Dog's story started before Vietnam and long before he joined the Marine Corps. It seems he was almost born with esprit de corps as part of his nature, and the circumstances of his life only served to enhance this tendency. Mad Dog as a child experienced near total external abuse that led to inner strength beyond explanation.

His defense of the underdog was natural because he was an underdog in life. Thus the name Mad Dog just seemed to happen. No one is really sure when he acquired it. Again and again society denied him justice; Divine Justice gave him inner strength and good . . . good for man, and good for God. For those who know him, this trait prevails today.

He was born during the Second World War in a small coal mining town known only for the coal it produced and the reputation of the people who mined it. His father was an Army private and served in the South Pacific. He had an older brother and sister and after his dad returned home, a younger brother was born.

For reasons unknown, Mad Dog was always the outcast of the children in the family. He received no gifts on holidays, no attention when ill or hurt, and no affection or attention from either parent.

A few months over the age of four, he began trying to earn his keep, earning a penny each time he dragged fire logs to the constant bonfire the grandpas of the town always seemed to keep going.

At the age of five, he got a job delivering papers. He got up early every day and walked for miles. His parents took no notice of his needs; so many miles were put on in the wintertime in shoes that had holes in the bottom. (These shoes, when his mother bought them for him, were so tight they made his feet bleed. He had to wear them anyway, as they were all he had, and by wintertime they had holes in the bottoms. Mad Dog soon learned that stuffing the soles of his shoes with paper helped keep out the wet a little longer.) He earned five cents a day at this job. His mother, saying that it was only right that he earn his keep, kept the money that he earned.

She also had a special brand of discipline for Mad Dog. Cursing at him, she would beat him with a cat-o'-nine-tails that she had come upon. She put tacks in the end of each cord, to make sure it did a proper job on him. He learned early that he would be blamed for everything that happened and would be beaten for it. He could not speak up to defend himself, as this just brought on a stronger rage from his mother. His father seemed indifferent to this treatment.

Shortly after his fifth birthday his mother left to "go to the city to work." Within two months she returned to gather up Mad Dog's sister and brothers and all the possessions in the house. She took everything and everyone. Everyone, that is, except Mad Dog. She left Mad Dog sitting under the high porch on one end of the coal patch home.

His younger brother Chuckie called out to him as he was dragged to the car. Mad Dog ran out from the porch, trying to "save" his brother but was stopped by his mother as she smacked him with a vicious blow in the face. Mad Dog, still trying to save his brother, gathered himself up and rushed at the car again. This time his mother's new male friend violently backhanded him to silence his calls to Chuckie. He flew to the ground in shock and pain, bleeding from the mouth and nose.

His mother's black car, followed by her boyfriend's truck, backed out of the driveway and left. Mad Dog sat up, hurt, frightened and confused. But he never shed a tear. He slowly got up and went to the bench under the high porch and sat to wait for his dad to return from the coal pit.

When Chuck senior came home, Mad Dog said, "Pap, she came and took Chuckie and Mary and Johnny."

His dad looked at him, his face black and angry. He slapped the child hard in the face. Mad Dog flew off the bench and landed in a heap. His mouth started to bleed again.

His dad entered the house and found an empty shell. All that was left was his clothes, some dirty dishes and dirty laundry in the basement where the washing machine had been. He walked over to the basement shower, undressed and took a shower.

Mad Dog's bleeding slowly stopped. He sat on the ground, bewildered and hurt, not knowing what to do, all alone.

In a small village news travels fast. Soon people were walking by the house just to look, as if in seeing the house they would somehow know what was going on. They chose to ignore the child on the ground.

Finally, an old "bubba" came and picked him up and said, "Come my little puppy, eat soup with bubba." Mad Dog held her hand in silence and walked to her home to be cleaned and fed.

In the mining patches during the forties, divorce was unheard of. It was something for Hollywood stars maybe, but not for "respectable" people who kept the old ways. Rejected by his mother and the product of a divorce, Mad Dog was the recipient of insults from children and adults alike. Taunts of "Don't play with him, he got no mother," or "Something must be wrong with him, even his mother didn't want him," contributed to Mad Dog's having to grow up tough.

And growing up tough meant Mad Dog had to face a difficult spiritual lesson as well. He discovered the hard way that God is not Santa Claus and does not act on deals. It all began one day when Mad Dog, a sad and lonely little boy, talked to God: "Dear God, please send my mommy and Chuckie and everybody home. Please."

Mad Dog continued, "God, I'll go to Sunday School every Sunday for a whole year if you send them home."

Mad Dog was true to his end of the "deal." The little five-year-old got himself ready each Sunday and in staunch determination that God would bring his mother back, walked the mile and a half to the school building where the services were held. Through rain and heat and snow Mad Dog stubbornly made his way to every Sunday School session, determined to win his goal.

It was the last Sunday of the year. Unwilling to face the futility of his deal, Mad Dog got himself ready for Sunday School. It had begun snowing the night before and there was over two feet of snow on the ground. To the five-year-old this looked like an almost impossible challenge. He stepped outside. The wind was howling and the windblown snow burnt his ears and whipped at his shoulders.

On he trudged, head bowed to the freezing wind, keeping his promise to God. The school ground was covered with drifting blowing snow, completely deserted. No one else had come. Not even the man who stood in as a pastor. Mad Dog waited all alone at the Sunday School door.

Finally a woman in a nearby house looked out the window and noticed the snow-covered little boy. She called to him to come to her house.

"Honey, nobody's going to come to Sunday School on a day like this! You ought to just go home." But Mad Dog was sure this was his day. He stood, expectantly peering out the window, for three hours. At last, defeated, he sadly slipped out the door.

Feeling abandoned by man and God, his tears freezing to his face, Mad Dog made his lonely trek home. That Sunday was the last time Mad Dog ever cried.

Mad Dog was tough, but he wasn't mean. He seemed to always be fighting, but not for himself, and he never started fights. Instead, he took to defending kids who were too small, or too weak or too frightened of the bigger kids to defend themselves.

But Mad Dog was quick and he was able, so for the most part, when kids gathered in the fields on the edge of the town, he was picked first for whatever sport was being played. He was often chosen even over kids four or five years older than himself. When winning was the idea, Mad Dog was always chosen to play.

Mad Dog excelled in sports. In high school he was a star football player, and won several full-time scholarships for football, this even though he was frequently not called on or used for plays that would have taken advantage of his athletic abilities.

Through the stigma of being left with his dad, Mad Dog had to develop a staunchly independent attitude. Other than with his father, he refused to be backed down by anyone who tried to bully him, either in action or in speech. Such an attitude was not commonplace in the fifties.

Although he could hit a baseball a mile, and run like a deer, he chose not to play baseball his senior year because the coach, who was the football coach as well, consistently displayed bad judgment in his directives and choices of players. Mad Dog, keenly aware of this, decided that listening to the inane bullshit that the coach considered superior coaching for two sports was more than he could handle.

Years later the coach admitted to Mad Dog that he was the best all-around football player the school had ever had. He added, "My last years of coaching, I'd have given a million bucks for a team of kids like you, but then your attitude was before your time." The old coach had wanted to make his peace before going to God, and this was his way of making restitution.

By the time he was a senior in high school, most of the kids had decided not to let the stigma of Mad Dog's home life interfere with friendship with him. Many adults also took notice that he cleaned the house, washed the clothes, cut grass for himself and his neighbors, taking only a glass of lemonade or water for pay from the elderly or infirm, and minimal donations of a nickel or sometimes a whopping fifty cents from the people he helped.

Although Mad Dog worked at various part-time jobs and was respectful of his elders, he was by no means a saint. He drank beer illegally with his buddies, getting a buzz on from a few bottles of beer. He was also somewhat in a state of constant horniness, which he relieved at every opportunity. However, he was not like most of the teenagers who bragged when they got laid or exaggerated feats of prowess.

When anyone asked him, he would always say, "I'm a virgin."

When his friends would protest, and said "Bullshit," he would say, "I'm not kidding you guys. I never touched her." No matter who the girl that they had brought up in the conversation, Mad Dog would always say, "I never touched her."

Mad Dog also spent several years working very hard on a farm. Walking to and from the farm was a little over three miles each way. When he wasn't participating in sports or on weekends when there were no sports activities, Mad Dog could always be counted on to show up at daybreak to work on the farm.

The farmer was a great influence on Mad Dog's life because of his honesty, integrity, and gentle, kind strength. Mad Dog had grown very loyal to the kind, hard-working man. When the farmer realized Mad Dog's situation at home, he volunteered to save Mad Dog's money for him until Mad Dog had enough to buy an old used car . . . the monumental amount of $100.

One night Mad Dog was driving his chariot to pick up some of his buddies so they could go to a dance in a nearby town. On his way, he happened to look into a store where some of the guys occasionally stopped in. He saw a fire inside.

He jammed on his brakes, leaped out and ran into the building to find two of the local boys holding two of the owner's sons while they burned buttons on the pinball machines. Mad Dog walked around the counter, got water, threw it on the fire and put it out.

He turned to the boys and told them to let the others go. They dared him to go get the police. Mad Dog really didn't want to, but they kept daring him to. So finally Mad Dog went outside.

A policeman, seeing Mad Dog's car parked in the road, pulled up behind the car. The owner's sons came running out and told the story of what had happened. The officer, after listening to the boys, turned to Mad Dog and said, "Okay, Dave. Tell me what really happened."

Mad Dog told what he had seen, and the officer then turned to the culprits.

"And what do you boys have to say?"

"We were just fooling around. We didn't mean nothin'."

The policeman said, "Get in the back of my car."

He turned to Mad Dog, told him to park his car and go along with him to the justice of the peace. They went to the magistrate's office with the owner's sons and the two boys who had set the fire.

The magistrate had the officer arrest Mad Dog. He said, "This kid Matthews is an accident waiting to happen."

The policeman said, "Sir, Matthews saved these two boys! He wasn't even there when all this started. He just happened to be passing by and saw the fire. Even these two actors admitted that young Dave didn't do anything wrong."

The owner's sons chimed in immediately.

"Dave saved us and put out the fires! These guys were choking us. He didn't do anything wrong!"

The magistrate refused to listen.

"I've heard enough! Take Matthews to jail right now, officer, or I'll call the state police."

Mad Dog was taken to jail and spent the night in a holding cell with murderers, rapists, and assorted other hoodlums, while the boys that actually did set the fire got off scot-free.

When Mad Dog was taken before the judge, the officer appeared to be a witness for him.

"This boy didn't do anything. He should be a hero instead of being in front of you, your honor."

The judge slammed his gavel down.

"Shut up! This is my court!"

Pointing his gavel at Mad Dog, he glowered, "You don't have a mother. You have two strikes against you. I should put you in jail, but I'll just put you on probation until you pay all the fines, court costs, and fire damage."

This in spite of the protestations of the police officer and the owner and his sons, who insisted that Mad Dog hadn't done anything, that he had, in fact, helped them. Mad Dog was convicted of a crime because, in the judge's words, he had two strikes against him because he didn't have a mother.

Mad Dog remembered the injustice of this all his life, and he always tried to sort things out to make sure he was never involved in an act, like the judge's, against an innocent person.

High school graduation night for most kids is a great party night. Mad Dog had gone out with his friends for the graduation celebration. He returned home in the wee hours of the morning to find his clothes in paper grocery bags on the front porch. He couldn't get in the house. The locks had been changed.

A note from his dad said, "Boy, you're out of school now. You got to make it on your own." No signature, no good wishes, just a good-bye in the only terms his dad could muster.

Mad Dog gathered the three bags and headed for the main and only street out of town.

Some of his buddies, seeing him, stopped and asked, "What the hell are you doing, Dog?"

Mad Dog's only reply was, "Can you guys take me to Union City?"

They rode in silence. The joy of the graduation had been tempered by the feeling that their buddy was somehow in dire straits. Looking out the window, Mad Dog saw the Marine recruiter's office. He said, "Let me off here."

His good friend Lou turned around and pulled in front of the darkened office. "Dog," he said, "come on home with me. My folks like you. Stay with us a couple of days. You got scholarships! Go to college, man!"

Another of the guys said, "You can stay with us. My dad said you can be an All-American if you go to college."

Mad Dog said, "Thanks, guys. I can't use you or get anyone else into my problems."

They decided to wait until the recruiter came in. Fortunately, he came in early. Mad Dog got out of the car and walked over to the recruiter.

"Can I sign up?" he asked.

The recruiter recognized him and queried, "Aren't you going to college?"

"I can't," Mad Dog said. "I guess I'll go somewhere else."

The recruiter said, "Come in. We'll test you right now."

Mad Dog and his buddies said good-bye. It was the last time he was to ever see some of them.

A NEW LIFE

Mad Dog took the written test and passed it with flying colors. He was sent to Pittsburgh for a physical, passed that with flying colors as well and was on a train to Parris Island that very night.

The greeting at Yamasse, gateway to Parris Island, was a shock for all. Arrivals from all over the East Coast were herded into ranks. Most everyone was ready to have a heart attack at the screaming and verbal intimidation. When the drill instructors told them to look straightforward, the raw recruits couldn't help but look at these men who sounded like raving maniacs. As they approached, only Mad Dog did not move his head or eyes. This didn't help either, as he too got yelled at.

The sergeant had, however, noted his obedience and put him in charge whenever the situation called for a recruit to be used in a supervisory capacity.

The organized mayhem of boot camp is something that even though described can only be really known by experiencing it. Take the haircuts, for instance . . . "How would you like it?" the barber says. "A little off the top and sides," the recruit answers. The electric clippers zip straight down the middle of the recruit's head almost to the scalp as cascades of hair fall to the floor or on the apron wrapped around him.

The delousings, the showers, the clothes and shoes thrown at them were also unexpected shocks. Although, unlike the cartoons and comedies, the fittings were done to the best degree possible. Even though it was done quickly, all the clothing was tried on prior to the recruit leaving the clothing supply building.

D.I.s (drill instructors) are normally the cream of the crop. They are the dedicated professionals who all but forsake family and friends when they have a platoon in training. Turning a pack of undisciplined youngsters into United States Marines is no easy task. Only rarely does a sadist slip through the cracks to make it through D.I. school, and occasionally a man snaps from the constant pressure.

The drill instructors organized programs to tear down each boy and then subtly rebuild him into a responsible man, and more than that, into a Marine who will be called upon to sacrifice his life for his beloved country and corps.

Basic things such as which is your left and which is your right are drilled into the recruits. Duties, such as fire watch (to sound the alarm if there is a fire while his brothers sleep), weapon cleaning, marksmanship, marching, discipline and teamwork are gone over again and again.

Part of the tearing down process is the feeling of helplessness. Many of the incidents that are so "horrible" at the time turn into funny stories as years go by. A few follow . . .

A favorite in the late fifties was to line the recruits up "asshole to belly button." This means simply what it says, i.e. the recruits are stuffed together pressing against each other "asshole to belly button."

With the recruits lined up this way, the D.I.s would stand in a doorway, one on each side and one in the middle, all three facing the recruit.

The D.I.s had one recruit stand at the door, and another fifteen or twenty feet away. The rest of the recruits were lined up out of earshot.

When the recruit in the doorway left, the one fifteen or twenty feet behind was to run up to replace him, then the front man of the "asshole to belly button" contingent was to run up and take his place.

Thus only the two recruits closest to the drill instructors could hear what the D.I.s said.

"Do you like your drill instructor?"

Recruit, "No, Sir!"

"You don't like your drill instructor? You ungrateful civilian son of a bitch!" The recruit is then slapped lightly and jostled about, then dismissed to the end of the line.

"Do you like your drill instructor?" is fired at the next man up.

Of course, the next recruit answers, "I like my drill instructor, Sir!"

The drill instructor then says, "Likin' leads to lovin'. Lovin' leads to huggin'. Huggin' leads to kissin'. Kissin' leads to fuckin'. You pervert, you want to fuck your drill instructors!" Then they beat him. The recruit never wins. No matter what, these games, silly as they seem at the time, are a necessary tool.

Marching . . .

The guidon (flag) of each platoon is their standard; it is used to show who they are. The platoons love to march. When things go well the drill instructors command them to shout their platoon number to show their pride in their platoon.

A great insult to a training platoon is to have their guidon furled (wrapped up and not flowing freely). The very worst insult is to have your platoon guidon carried furled and upside down.

The platoon Mad Dog was in had been training only a few weeks and were still marching "the numbers," i.e. drill instructor, "Left face." The entire platoon calls, "One," turning to the left, then "Two," bringing the right foot to its proper position.

A sharp platoon "outposting" (leaving for infantry training that week) marched by, the seventy-five heels hitting the grinder (parade ground) as one, every movement like a finely-tuned machine as they marched by. The raw recruits almost drooled and to a man, lost their concentration watching the "real" Marines march by.

The drill instructor said, "So you shit maggots like that, huh?"

"Yes, sir!" they answered.

"You think you can march like that?"

"Yes, sir!" the recruits screamed, hoping somehow they would be able to look as sharp as the graduating Marines.

The drill instructor said, "Attention," paused, "forward, march."

This was the last command most of the men got correct. The drill instructor started giving commands that the newcomers had never heard.

"By the left flank, march."

"Right oblique, march."

"Forward, march."

"To the rear, march."

After one minute, the platoon was spread out across the drill field in total disarray. The drill instructor barked, "Okay! Okay! Stop! Not halt, stop. Halt's a command for marching. You shit birds aren't marching! You're out roaming around like a bunch of barnyard animals. Now get back here and fall into three ranks. Do it! Move it! Move! Move! Move!" the drill instructor shouted. "Count off by fives."

The recruits counted. It took them several tries to get it right.

The senior drill instructor then said, "Okay, girls, all ones, moo like a cow. All twos, baa like a sheep. All threes, quack like a duck. All fours, cluck like a chicken. All fives, heehaw like a donkey. Now get in a herd. You ain't people, you're animals."

The recruits were put into a round herd, asshole to belly button. The guidon was wrapped up and tied, given to the guide and he was ordered to carry it upside down.

The guide strutted proudly in front, while behind him came the herd of braying, mooing, clucking, baaing, quacking men, totally humiliated, while all the other platoons were halted to watch the spectacle as the recruits were herded back to their barracks.

Their attention span immediately improved as did performance of duties.

Night prayers . . . there was supposedly one hour of "free" time each evening. The drill instructor told the recruits what could be accomplished in "free" time, so in fact this free time was an extension of the day's work. Cleaning rifles, shining boots (shoes had not been issued), polishing brass, reading the guide book and if the men were brave, a quick letter or two were among the choices for free time.

On first arrival the men were ordered to write home. Mad Dog wrote the one letter that was ordered and never another, so he was only too happy to do what the drill instructor had suggested.

One night the recruits got a little antsy and were making noise. The drill instructor crept in to see who the culprits were. He noted Mad Dog cleaning his rifle.

The drill instructor crept back to the door and made his proper entrance. A recruit saw him enter this time and yelled, "Attention!" All of the recruits dropped what they were doing and came to attention.

The drill instructor immediately started screaming.

"You fucking shit maggots don't have enough to do. You skylarking pack of split-tail maggots are making more fucking noise than a company of real Marines."

He then approached Mad Dog. The drill instructor knew Mad Dog was an exceptional recruit, but he wanted to test him.

"Matthews, was that you making all that noise?"

"No, sir."

"Who was it?"

"Private Matthews doesn't know, sir."

The drill instructor seemed to go berserk yet he was in total control.

"You lying fucking maggot! You tell me who it was or I'll have your ass! Spit it out, you turd!"

Mad Dog stood ramrod straight, looked straight ahead and said, "Sir, the private does not know who was making noise."

The drill instructor wanted to test not only Mad Dog but the guilty ones as well.

He said to Mad Dog, calmer now, "Maybe God will tell you if you pray awhile, Private. Now put that weapon together and stow your gear."

Mad Dog quickly accomplished this and returned to attention.

The drill instructor, looking half insane, loudly said, "Since you won't report those cowardly shit birds to your drill instructor, you start praying Marine Corps style. Put your toes on the top rack (bunk)." Mad Dog did this with little difficulty, his hands supporting him on the deck (floor).

The drill instructor then said, "Put your elbows on the deck and clasp your hands behind your head." Mad Dog did this easily, but as time wore on his elbows became sore. He scooted around, trying in vain to be comfortable. Each move skinned his elbows and droplets of blood began oozing from them.

The barracks was quiet now. The drill instructor returned to turn the lights out for the night.

He approached Mad Dog and said, "Private, has God told you who was making all that racket? If he hasn't you can stay here all night."

The drill instructor knew Mad Dog would not report the offenders. He hoped the guilty parties would confess to get their buddy out of the mess he was in because of them. No one moved or spoke.

The drill instructor said, "Okay. All you maggots get in your racks except Matthews."

The recruits got into their bunks and the drill instructor turned off the lights and he walked out. He was planning to return in a few minutes to send Mad Dog to bed, still hoping the guilty parties would confess.

Just then, out of nowhere came the officer of the day making his tour. He said, "Sergeant, let's take a walk around your squad bay."

The drill instructor had no choice but to say "Yes, sir" and follow the captain. Upon entering the squad bay the officer almost immediately spotted Mad Dog's diagonal form.

He turned on his flashlight and walked at a quick pace to the suspended private and said, "What the hell are you doing, Private?"

"Praying, sir."

"Get on your feet, Private."

Mad Dog jumped to his feet and stood at attention.

The captain said, "Were you being punished, Private?"

"No, sir. Private Matthews was praying, sir."

The captain said, "If this is true, I apologize for interrupting a religious ceremony, but lights out means you have to get into your rack."

The drill instructor, seeing an opening, said, "I told you, Matthews, you hit the rack when lights out comes. Now hit it!"

Mad Dog said, "Yes, sir," and got gratefully into his bunk.

The officer and the drill instructor left and as peaceful sleep came to Mad Dog he heard the captain ask, "What kind of odd-ball religion is that recruit?"

A NEW CHALLENGE

The hectic pace of boot camp soon erased the thought of that night in Mad Dog's mind. As the raw recruits started to shape up in body, mind and spirit one wouldn't recognize them from the first weeks of training.

One day, a border line recruit named McGrath kept a live round of ammunition from marksmanship practice on the rifle range. Mad Dog saw him slip it into his pocket but did not have a chance to approach him until they were marched back to the barracks. As soon as they were dismissed Mad Dog got McGrath's squad leader and briefed him on what he had seen.

They approached McGrath at his bunk and his squad leader, Tinsley, spoke.

"Mac, I think you accidentally picked up a live round. Let's have it."

McGrath, who was a head taller than Tinsley and Mad Dog, swung his big right hand and connected on Tinsley's jaw, sending him sprawling.

McGrath said to Mad Dog, "I've been waiting for a chance to nail you, Matthews. Now you're mine."

He barely got "mine" out when Mad Dog hit him hard and fast with a flurry of punches that put Mac against the bunks, dazed.

Mad Dog grabbed him by the lapels and said, "Cough it up, asshole. Give me that live round."

The three drill instructors, who had been watching the scene unbeknownst to the recruits, burst in to the shouts of "attention" by the men in the platoon.

"What's going on here, Matthews?" the senior D.I. asked.

"Private Matthews adjusting Private McGrath's uniform, sir," Mad Dog said.

"And I suppose that red stuff coming out of his mouth and nose is some sort of camouflage paint," the D.I. countered.

Tinsley was now on his feet, still groggy.

The drill instructor, never taking his eyes off McGrath, asked, "Tinsley, what's going on?"

Before Tinsley could speak, a short baby-faced Marine said, "Sir, Private Yuli requests permission to speak to the drill instructor."

"Speak," the D.I. said.

"Sir, Private McGrath has a live round and he sucker-punched Tinsley when he asked for it. Private Matthews saved Tinsley's ass from getting stomped."

The drill instructor looked at McGrath and said, "You got a live round, boy?"

McGrath said, "No, sir."

The D.I. said, "Face your rack and put your hands on it. Spread your legs."

One of the junior drill instructors moved behind McGrath to pat him down and with the first pat said, "What's in here, Private?"

McGrath said, "Nothing, sir."

"Empty your pockets," the D.I. said.

McGrath brought out the live round and said, "Tinsley or Matthews planted this on me."

The senior D.I. told the other junior D.I. to go to the office and call the M.P.s. The M.P.s quickly arrived and took McGrath away.

The senior D.I. asked Tinsley, "Are you okay, Private? Do you need to go to sick bay?"

Tinsley replied, "Private Tinsley is fine, sir."

333

The drill instructor said, "How did you know that McGrath had a round, Private?"

"Sir, Private Matthews told me and we wanted to get it before we had a problem."

The drill instructor looked at Mad Dog and said, "Is that true, Private Matthews?"

Mad Dog had to say, "Yes, sir."

The drill instructor said, "Clean your weapons and get ready for chow."

The three D.I.s left the recruits to attend to the weapons and they returned to their office. The whole platoon of trainees were on edge over the excitement of the day and the drill instructors all stayed during the free time to keep them calm and acting almost human.

The next morning as the men were falling into ranks after breakfast, a runner (messenger) approached the senior D.I., spoke softly and briefly, and was off again back to where he had come from.

When all the platoon had assembled the senior D.I. said, "You people will be with Gunny Sergeant Delvecco temporarily. You will obey him as if it were your regular drill instructor."

A gunnery sergeant that the men had never seen approached; the three regular D.I.s left, walking to the barracks.

The gunnery sergeant said, "Private Matthews, report to your drill instructors at the duty hut now. Dismissed."

Mad Dog said, "Aye, aye, sir," and was off on the double to the drill instructors' office. He reported by beating hard three times on the door frame.

"Speak," said a voice from inside.

"Sir, Private Matthews reporting as ordered."

"What are your orders, Private?"

"Report to the drill instructors, sir."

"Center." Mad Dog centered himself in the doorway by taking a neat crisp step and executing a perfect left-face to be looking into the office.

"Private, do you know where battalion headquarters is?"

"Yes, sir," said Mad Dog. He knew because the platoon had marched by it many times and it was between the barracks and the mess hall.

"Report to the battalion commander's office, Private. Put on a clean uniform and walk, don't run there, understand?"

"Yes, sir," Mad Dog answered.

"Dismissed."

Mad Dog stepped back and did a sharp about-face and went to his locker to get a clean set of utilities (the Marine work uniform).

The drill instructors arrived at the headquarters office. In the office was the lieutenant colonel (battalion commander), the chaplain, and Mad Dog's company commander.

The first sergeant spoke, "Colonel, here are the drill instructors that you wanted to see."

The colonel said, "Thank you, First Sergeant. I'd like you to stay here."

"Yes, sir," the first sergeant said and took a seat.

The three drill instructors reported and stood at attention. The colonel said, "At ease, men. The chaplain has serious charges against you three of beating a recruit . . . " He looked down at his desk. "Matthews. Private McGrath said you beat him and that you three have all beaten this Private Matthews. I'm going to talk to him and let you know if there will be charges."

There was a knock at the door and the colonel said, "Yes."

The door opened and a staff sergeant said, "Private Matthews was told to report here, Colonel."

The colonel said, "Send him in," and to the drill instructors, "You men wait outside. I'll send for you when I need you."

The three came to attention, said, "Yes, sir," and left.

Mad Dog was truly nervous for the first time when he was escorted in by the sergeant who had announced his arrival. He stood at attention.

The colonel said, "At ease, Private. Have a seat." The colonel motioned to some empty chairs on his right. While seated here, Mad Dog would be looking at the other occupants of the room.

The colonel offered a cigarette. Mad Dog, who didn't smoke, was so uncomfortable that he accepted. When the first sergeant brought matches, Mad Dog nervously took another cigarette and actually had two lit at once.

"No need to be afraid or nervous, son. You're not in trouble. The chaplain here had a report that your drill instructors have hit you and other members of your platoon. Is that true?"

Mad Dog instantly replied, "No, sir!"

The chaplain said, "Son, you've got to tell the truth. These things aren't allowed."

Mad Dog said, "Sir, I've never been hit and I never saw anybody else hit by my drill instructors."

"What about poor Private McGrath?" the chaplain said.

"McGrath's a shit bird, sir. I hit him, not the drill instructors."

"You, Private? Why, how could you hit your buddy?" the milquetoast chaplain asked.

"Beggin' the Padre's pardon, but Mac ain't my buddy. He's a big ass shit bird. He brought a live round off the range and I waffled him. The drill instructors didn't know anything about this, sir."

The colonel said, "Will you sign a statement to that effect, Private?"

"Yes, sir," Mad Dog said.

The colonel turned and said, "First Sergeant, have the statement typed and send the drill instructors in."

The first sergeant said, "Yes, sir," to the colonel and "Come with me," to Mad Dog.

Mad Dog got up and followed the first sergeant into the hallway. The three drill instructors were waiting. The first sergeant winked and said, "The colonel wants to see you."

The D.I.s knew from the wink that Mad Dog had not ratted on them. They reported to the colonel, who said, "There is no evidence of any wrongdoing. Report to your platoon. Private Matthews is signing a statement in your favor. A copy will be sent to each of you as soon as he's signed it and it's witnessed." He added, "Any questions, Captain?"

"No, sir," the captain answered.

"You are all dismissed," the colonel said, and the D.I.s, the chaplain and the captain left the office.

In the hallway the captain said, "Come to my office. I'll fill you in while the statement is typed."

The captain told the three drill instructors the story that Mad Dog had told and used the same language. The D.I.s were amused, but still had to keep their composure and plan how to keep Mad Dog from getting a swelled head. They walked back to their office and hatched a plan.

Mad Dog signed the statements and was told to report to his platoon. He ran back to his barracks and reported in the usual manner to the D.I.'s hut (office).

"Sir, Private Matthews reporting as ordered." This was usual procedure, but what was unusual was the drill instructors invited him into the hut to sit down.

They had the statement in hand. The senior D.I. asked Mad Dog, "Did you sign this, Private Matthews?"

"Yes, sir."

"Private, do you know you can get thrown into the brig for signing false statements? This is an official document, Private. You lied."

Whatever air was in Mad Dog's sails quickly left.

The senior drill instructor said, "Get out of my sight, you lying shit maggot!"

Mad Dog, in a daze, said, "Yes, sir," and was out the door.

The platoon was just entering the barracks and Mad Dog ran to his bunk and stood at attention. The D.I.s were grateful, but could not show it. Mad Dog had saved three careers, and felt deep inner satisfaction. He slept like a baby again that night.

PIECES OF WAR

Pieces of war: . . . insanity . . . bravery . . . ingenuity . . . sadness . . . pathos.

The Real Thing . . .

The sun beat down on the beautiful white Hawaiian beach as the off-duty Marines relaxed and talked.

One of the men turned as he spoke, "Did you hear they're sending some battalions from Kaneohe Bay to somewheres called Vietnam?"

"What the hell is Vietnam?"

"I dunno, but I heard there was a transfer of several of the battalions there within the last few days."

Just then a car pulled up in the parking lot with four more Marines who had just come from the base.

"Hey, you shit birds, anybody want to get combat pay?" one of the occupants yelled.

It was James White II, a black corporal called Whitey 2X by his friends and only his friends. Also in the car were Joe Williams, a lance corporal, and a super intelligent half-Blackfoot Indian by the name of John Nebson. As the four got out of the car and walked to the group, questions were flung faster than anyone could answer or understand.

"Slow down! White man too many forked tongues wagging for me to understand," Joe shot at them.

Willie Miter spoke up and said, "What's going on, John?"

"They just asked for volunteers to go to Vietnam to chase dit-ties and run DF equipment," John replied. "Captain Riffen is tak-ing a planeload of equipment and men out in the morning. He wanted us, so we all volunteered," Nebson added.

"Anybody seen Smokey?"

"Why do you want him?" asked one of the men.

"If I gotta go, so does that screwball. I can't leave him with all these loose women floating around!" John answered as the entire contingent broke out in laughter.

The next morning the equipment was being put aboard a KC-130 as the Marines were milling around. The gathered men were told to prepare to board the aircraft and dismissed. The total advanced contingent was forty-eight: forty-six enlisted men and two officers. The planes landed in Okinawa later the same day and the men were given a liberty to carouse one more time prior to going to Nam.

The next day they loaded up and flew the final lap to Da Nang airfield in the Republic of South Vietnam. As they unloaded, what the Marines noticed first when the plane doors opened was the heat, not the ideal weather for a bunch of hung over Gyrenes. It almost took their breath away. When their eyes adjusted to the bright glare, their stomachs turned and they gulped as they tried to tune in to the officer welcoming them to the R.V.N. As they looked around, their hearts pounded at the realization that they were in the war.

The jets were parked in open bunkers, each in its own little cavern. Fighters and bombers were taking off constantly. Transport and supply planes landed between take-offs. A pile of ponchos with something in them was stacked to one side of a small building. (Later they learned these were the bodies of men who would never see the States again.)

Each group of Marines was assigned to certain outfits as replacements or, as in their case, left waiting until they were picked up by someone from their headquarters for assignment. A jeep followed by a 3/4-ton truck pulled up and out jumped a captain who called to Captain Riffin. Riffin wasn't sure he knew him until he approached a little closer. It was Captain Raye, an old friend. He had changed. He looked fifty years old, and he was only twenty-six. He spoke with Captain Riffin a few minutes, telling him that they would relieve a platoon that was relatively safe, but had been decimated by dysentery and malaria. He filled him in on the rest of the details, then hopped back into the jeep.

When Captain Raye arrived back at headquarters, he spotted Gunnery Sergeant Clarke. He yelled for him to come over and got out of the jeep. As Oop walked over, the captain headed for a more private section, pulled out his cigarettes and offered Oop one.

"Now Captain, you shouldn't be trying to get me to have more vices," Oop kidded as he declined the smokes. They both chuckled as they stopped and turned toward each other.

"Oop, I got you and Mad Dog transferred to my company from the advisors. I'm going to send you out with Captain Riffin. He's okay, but has no combat experience."

"Whatever you say, Cap'n."

They drove to where the new arrivals were. Captain Raye introduced Captain Riffin and Oop. "Oop has been here with the advisors. I'll give him to you for awhile. I need four teams of four men each, at least one N.C.O. with each team. The rest of us will remain in Da Nang and set up headquarters."

"Oop, you are going in the field as platoon sergeant with the four recon teams. Get your equipment and men together. You've got to be in position tonight."

Captain Raye then left in his jeep.

Meanwhile Captain Riffin approached his sergeant. "I was informed by Captain Raye that since us guys came in daylight, we will probably get probed at least, tonight. No flares are to be set out. The sneaky little bastards will just steal them, and our men may be depending on the flares for a warning. That's a sure way to get our asses waxed. If we're hit early we can expect harassment all night. Trust no one, he said."

"Aye Aye, Cap'n," the sergeant answered as he saluted and walked toward the men to move them out.

Captain Riffin went with the weakest team in his estimation to an artillery group south of Da Nang so that if there were any targets he had easy access to bring artillery fire to bear. When all of the teams were at their locations and radio contact was established, Captain Riffin walked to the Army commander's tent to let him know that they were operational.

"Tell your squad leaders to keep half of the men on alert all night," he was instructed. It didn't take long for Captain Riffin to realize this advice wasn't necessary. Charlie kept them awake . . . or dead.

Night drew on. The troops were grab-assing and only a little bit nervous. "Hell," one of them said, "this ain't war. This is just like Hawaii . . . camping out!"

At 23:30 (11:30) they started to take small arms fire.

After the first round, seven Marines were dead, and nine wounded. Captain Riffin was killed in the first fire. The radio man had been hit in the leg, but he ignored his wounds and stuck close to Oop while trying to raise headquarters for help.

The sounds of battle and screaming wounded permeated the air, mingled with Charlie yelling that the Marines' wives were sleeping with draft dodgers. The corpsmen rushed to gather the wounded together in a safer place to protect them, and separated the dead, wrapping them in their ponchos. The absolute look of terror on the faces of the men was enough to indicate that they knew the camping was over and they were in the war.

Green Beret Style Hospitality . . .

The company was on their way to Khe Sanh, to a Green Beret encampment located in the area. (Khe Sanh became newsworthy later as a Marine base where a heroic stand was made against the North Vietnamese.)

One night, while en route, Oop, Mad Dog and their platoon were on a perimeter watch near the jungle. Several hours after dark they heard noises as though the jungle brush were being moved constantly. There was no firing, just the rustling that continued off and on all through the night. At first light they went to investigate. They found a horse with a broken leg.

"Whadda ya know, it's a three-legged horse," Mad Dog exclaimed. "I guess they just left it. What do ya think we should do with it?"

"Let's just take it along. Maybe somebody at the camp will think of something," Oop suggested.

They tied a rope around its neck and took the horse with them to the Green Beret camp. The commanding officer spotted them and made his way over.

"We'll outfit you guys with Thompson submachine guns and ammo in trade for that horse," he offered.

Oop and Mad Dog looked at each other in surprise.

Oop grinned. "You got a deal. What are you going to do with a horse with a broken leg?"

The C.O. spoke casually, "My men will take care of it."

That night the Marines were invited to a barbecue. The Green Berets had cooked up a feast, and the Marines were treated to an absolutely delicious meal. It turned out that the Green Berets had barbecued the horse. In this case it was an act of kindness for the horse as well as a treat for the unsuspecting men.

Green Berets are trained much more intensely on various aspects of survival than regular Army troops. The C.O. immediately recognized that the horse with a broken leg was untreatable, and that it would only suffer and die a slow painful death. He humanely ordered the horse shot. But he had also instantly recognized another use for it, and ordered that it be butchered.

Contrary to popular belief, the horse meat was delicious. The barbecue and comradery provided one of the best meals and best times most of the men had in Vietnam! Oop and Mad Dog congratulated one another on their lucky find and the entire platoon had new respect for the U.S. Army, and especially the Green Berets.

The Invisible Highway (Ho Chi Minh Trail) . . .

Using the Green Beret camp as a home base, Mad Dog and Oop took a squad-size reconnaissance patrol out. They had certain objectives, as did several other squads. They had been specifically told to check out an area several miles away from the camp. When they neared it, they heard the unmistakable sound of motor vehicles where there was not supposed to be a road.

Oop said to Mad Dog, "Take three men and recon ahead. We'll wait here."

Mad Dog turned to his men, "You three snoopers and poopers come on with me. No grab-assing! See ya later, Oop."

They quietly crept forward and found where the noise was coming from.

One of Mad Dog's men whispered aloud, "What the fu . . . " as Mad Dog's hand clamped over his mouth to silence him.

The incredible sight before them numbed their senses temporarily, much like when someone gets their first closeup view of the Grand Canyon. There before them was an old roadway which must have been constructed while the French were still in Vietnam, made of logs from felled trees. The limbs of the trees on both sides of the road had been laced and woven together to form a perfect and natural camouflage over the log road. It was one of the most incredibly ingenious things Mad Dog had ever seen.

They fell back to Oop's position and radioed what they had found. The radio operator had to encode the message and, after repeating it three times, Oop was ordered by headquarters to the radio.

"Boxer, this is Boxer 44," Oop spoke into the handset.

"Forty-four, is this information reliable? Over."

"Boxer, the Dog reported it. Over."

"Forty-four, okay, go with it. Keep us posted. Boxer, out."

"Roger. Out."

Oop told his men what Mad Dog had found.

He added, "We are gonna to have to be extra careful. This is one of the biggest finds of the war. We'll take our time to scope it out. Everyone take a good look to get it out of your system, but be quiet! I don't want them to know we're on to them. Then we're gonna follow it south to see what we can find. H.Q. is going to send another squad north to see how far it goes."

After only several miles the road ended. They could see North Vietnamese unloading supplies from the trucks onto bicycles, which would be used to peddle the supplies much further south on smaller trails. They were also loading supplies onto horses and elephants being used as pack animals to resupply areas closer to this part of the Ho Chi Minh Trail. The trucks then returned north on the invisible wooden highway. (Later, after many recon missions, it was discovered that this secret, totally concealed highway was several hundred miles long. It was connected by underground tunnels to supply depots in North Vietnam.)

The Phantom Pilot . . .

The company was on duty around the small dirt airstrip at Dong Ha. Some of the men were listening to radios. Hanoi Hannah could be heard, and Radio Singapore, which played up-to-date music. The theme song playing that day, that still rings in many ears to this day when Vietnam is mentioned, was the theme from *A Summer Place*.

A few men were listening to the pilots chatter as they bombed over North Vietnam. One of the men listening to the pilots' chatter, suddenly looked up and yelled, "Somebody better get Mad Dog and Oop! This fly boy's gonna have his navigator punch out. He has a missile up one engine. It didn't explode. I think he's gonna try to land it here!"

One of the men went running out to where Oop and Mad Dog had their tent pitched and babbled out the story. As they were listening, a corporal came running from headquarters saying, "The captain wants to see you right away! A navigator from an F-4 is going to bail out. He wants us to help protect him and get him back here."

The man who had run for Mad Dog said, "That's what I wanted you guys to hear!"

Mad Dog went running to where the men were around the radio, which was only a short distance. He said, "All right, grab your rifles and some ammo. We're gonna protect this guy!"

It was already too late. The navigator had bailed out and was slowly drifting down only a few hundred yards from the edge of the airstrip. He was going to make a perfect landing in the midst of the Marines, who were all out in awe. He didn't need any protection! He was just going to be escorted to headquarters so that he could get a ride back.

The pilot, meanwhile, made a teardrop turn and came back in to try to land on the dirt airstrip. An Air Force Phantom, for those who are not familiar with the airplane, is a two-seater with two engines. The missile, which had been intended to down the plane, had hit and lodged in one of the engines. The young pilot, when he realized what had happened, shut down that engine and ordered the navigator to bail out. He was going to try to bring the plane in for landing.

Dong Ha was the closest airstrip. It wasn't made for jets. It wasn't long enough and it was dirt. The pilot wasn't sure—no one was sure—that the landing would not explode the missile. The Marines collectively held their breath and said silent prayers that the missile wouldn't explode before they got the pilot out.

He landed smoothly, but this airstrip was much too short. This pilot had guts! He kept the jet under control and steered it straight on down. It went off the end of the runway. The ground was soggy and slowed the jet down a little. It went down one hill and straight up another, finally stopping.

The canopy opened and the Marine Air Wing men stationed at the strip, who were already running to help him, hurriedly pulled him out of the cockpit and away from the plane.

Having gotten the officer and themselves away from the plane, they waited and watched. When they were sure the missile was not going to explode from the impact, they sent out experts to disarm the missile and extract it.

Oop, Mad Dog and the other men who had witnessed the whole scene were in awe at the bravery of this young officer who had brought the plane in safely. It was one of the many unbelievable things that they witnessed in Vietnam.

Later on in the day, the Air Force sent a huge, what can only be described as a workhorse helicopter with a winch and cable. The plane was secured to it and flown, carried back by the big workhorse, to Da Nang for repairs.

B-52 . . .

Things were slow, and the captain had been alerted that the company could send some men out to an Air Force base in the Philippines for quick two- and three-day R and Rs. He was considering who to send first, and since Oop and Mad Dog had by this time been in the country over fifteen months, he wondered if they would want to go. He approached Oop and made him the offer. Oop quickly accepted.

As Oop entered Mad Dog's quarters, he said, "Dog, get yourself ready. We're going to the Philippines for a two-day drunk!" Mad Dog wasted no time getting some clothes in his genuine PX-bought overnight bag, and they were soon off.

When they got there Oop looked up some of his old buddies and they made arrangements to take time off. Somehow in the process, Mad Dog and a master sergeant that Oop knew got separated from the rest of the group.

The master sergeant, quaffing the last of his drink, turned to Mad Dog with a crooked grin.

"Do you want to play B-52?" he queried.

Mad Dog, always ready for action, said, "Sure. How do ya play B-52?"

"Let's climb a coconut tree and we'll bomb the cars going by."

So the two pie-eyed Marines climbed two trees close together and noisily began hurling coconuts at passing cars.

The master sergeant took the first shot. He quaffed a swig of whiskey, picked a coconut, took aim and let fire.

"Bombs away!" he yelled as he threw the coconut.

Mad Dog took a swig, and cheered him on. Then he grabbed a coconut and yelled, "Here, sucker. Take this!" and threw his coconut at a passing car.

The cars were in no real danger of being hit, because the Marines had carried an ample supply of liquid refreshment with them up the trees. But the flying coconuts and the raucous language drew plenty of attention. Word spread throughout the bar that two nuts were in trees throwing coconuts at passing cars. Oop immediately knew one of them had to be Mad Dog.

When they were reported, which didn't take long, the Air Force base responded by sending fire trucks with cherry pickers to get the men down.

An Air Force captain arrived at the scene and pompously ordered the men to the ground. He was answered by an invitation to come and get them and a round of coconuts. He decided to try to reason with them. Finally the two were coaxed into coming down. The master sergeant was the first to go.

Mad Dog whispered, "When you get down, I'll start throwing more coconuts. You try to get away so you won't have a mark on your record. I don't give a shit!"

So as planned, when the master sergeant hit the ground, Mad Dog started hurling coconuts again and the top made his getaway. The Air Force captain, dodging coconuts, renewed his efforts to reason with Mad Dog. After a few minutes, when he was sure his friend was out of sight, Mad Dog calmed down.

He said, "Okay, send up a cherry picker. I'll come down.

So they sent it up. He got on board and they brought him down.

The captain said, "You're under arrest. Let me see your I.D."

Just then a man in civilian clothes stepped forward and glowered at Mad Dog.

"You've finally done it this time, boy! I've been waiting for you to fuck up! I'm going to put you in the brig for ten years!"

As he spoke he waved a threatening finger in Mad Dog's face.

The Air Force captain asked, "Do you know this man, sir?" Immediately assuming the man in civilian clothes was an officer.

The man, with a triumphant look replied, "Yes, I do! I've been waiting for a chance to lock him up!"

The Air Force captain smiled smugly.

"I'll release him to your custody, sir!"

The man in civilian clothes said, "Thank you, Captain! I'll see that there's a commendation in this for you."

The Air Force captain smiled as Mad Dog was led away by the arm, being brow-beaten.

"You shit bird! You're going to jail now! I've been waiting for this!"

Finally, they got to the car and Mad Dog was roughly shoved in. There, grinning at him, were Oop and several of his other drinking buddies.

Oop, nodding his head toward the man in civilian clothes, looked at Mad Dog and said, "Gunnery sergeant. Friend of mine."

The "officer" in civilian clothes turned around to the Air Force men, flipped them the bird, and hollered, "Fuck you, fly guys!"

He hopped in the car and they took off. The Air Force men jumped in their car and quickly turned it around, but the escapees, laughing and whooping and hollering, had disappeared around the bend. Mad Dog and the master sergeant, thanks to Oop's quick thinking, had escaped scot-free.

God's Play . . .

The next morning, after the B-52 game, sober and saner heads and minds prevailed. It was decided that Oop and Mad Dog would be best served by staying on the Marine base rather than carousing, because the A.P.s, M.P.s, and S.P.s all would probably be on the lookout for Mad Dog.

One of the gunnery sergeants said, "Com'on with me. I have tear gas training today."

So they put on their Marine utilities and waited for the gunnery sergeant to get his men loaded in trucks to be taken to the area where the tear gas training was to take place. He popped his head into Mad Dog and Oop's area, and said, "Let's go, you guys," and they were off. They got into the back of a jeep. There was a Marine lieutenant in the passenger's side and Gunny Woods (the friend of Oop's who had invited them). Gunny Woods introduced the lieutenant to Mad Dog and Oop.

"Sergeant, this is Oop and Mad Dog. Oop is an old buddy of mine. They're here for a few days' leave from Vietnam." He turned to the men and said, "Lieutenant Jones is my platoon commander."

The lieutenant was very congenial and asked them, "What's your M.O.S.?"

Oop answered, "We both have several M.O.S.s, but right now we are 0-three genuine USMC-issue grunts!"

All four chuckled at Oop's answer.

The lieutenant said, "It would be great if you both would participate and observe our training while you're here. It may save a few lives when these guys get to Nam."

Gunny Woods interjected, "Today is tear gas training, sir. But if they are still here tomorrow we can put them to work if they want."

When they arrived at the tear gas training site, the men were already there. The gunnery sergeant called them to attention and ran briefly over the exercise. As he was speaking, the sergeant in charge of the tear gas exercise came out and recognized Mad Dog. He had also been an advisor in Vietnam, however he had only been there three months before stepping on a punji stick and forced to leave the country. He walked over to Mad Dog and they exchanged greetings; then he said hello to the others.

He proposed, "Why don't we all go in and we'll sing the 'Marine Corps Hymn' without masks and show these men what real Marines are!" Oop and Mad Dog weren't in the mood for this silliness, but the invitation was extended so loudly that they felt they had to.

The exercise consisted of groups of men with their gas masks on, going into the building, the tear gas being released, and then removing their mask for about ten seconds, after which they could leave the building.

One gunnery sergeant, who had not been to Vietnam, overheard the loudly proclaimed request, and in a high squeaky voice said, "Com'on, you guys. I'll go with you!" Neither Oop or Mad Dog knew him, but the sergeant said in a low voice, "This guy's a good guy. But he has the damnedest voice!"

Again the gunnery sergeant squeaked shrilly, "Com'on, Marines!"

So Oop, Mad Dog, the instructor, and the gunnery sergeant entered the building. The first group of men came in with their gas masks on. The sergeant released the tear gas, the room quickly filled. The eyes of the four without masks began burning. Some of the men with gas masks were panicking, but they were fine and protected by the gas masks.

Then the sergeant yelled, "Take 'em off!"

A few of the men instantly took them off, some hesitated. He quickly moved around and said, "Take 'em off!" and started to help them. They took them off, coughing.

He screamed, "Don't rub your eyes! Don't rub your eyes!"

And then he yelled, "Okay you guys, let's show them how real Marines do it!" And at that, the four men who had entered without masks, sang the "Marine Corps Hymn" bellowing out the words as best they could. By then the sergeant who had gone in with Oop and Mad Dog was coughing violently. The instructor grabbed him and led him to the door, opened it, and said, "Okay, men. File out in an orderly fashion."

Oop and Mad Dog were the next ones out. For some reason, the gunnery sergeant who had gone in with them was walking stiff-legged with his arms almost directly out at his sides, like some B-movie monster. As he was walking around the area, the men watching him fell into hysterics.

He numbly headed for some trees. Then suddenly—as if aimed by an unseen power—a coconut broke loose from one of the trees, came hurtling directly down and hit him on top of the head, knocking him colder than a mackerel. He fell like he had been walking, his stiff legs and arms spread wide apart.

Right then the company commander pulled up . . . just in time to witness the fall. "What the hell is going on here?" he asked in astonishment.

No one could answer him. Everyone was buckled over in laughter. The lieutenant who had ridden out with Oop and Mad Dog tried unsuccessfully to explain. He would start to talk, and then burst out laughing again.

After a few minutes, he got control of himself, and was able to tell the company commander what had happened. The captain, looking at the sprawled-out gunnery sergeant, couldn't help but laugh too. A few moments later the gunnery sergeant sat up and looked around blankly, rubbing his sore head.

"What the hell happened to me?" he squeaked in his shrill voice.

They buckled over helpless with laughter again. Their guffaws were so infectious that they got him, looking confused, laughing too. He sat on the ground holding his stomach with one hand laughing—he wasn't exactly sure at what—and rubbing his head wondering about the tremendous headache that had suddenly come on.

Business As Usual . . .

The company was on a patrol walking along a road adjacent to rice paddies, and the Vietnamese were planting. One of the women bent over near one of the dikes, and a snake bit her on the cheek. She screamed out in terror.

The Marines, who were past her about a hundred yards when this happened, went running back thinking that she had stepped on a punji stick. By the time they got there the other farmers had her lying down on the dike. A corpsman quickly ran forward and one of the Vietnamese, with two fingers hooked, made the sign of a snake striking. The corpsman didn't have any antivenom. The woman began to convulse and died while the Marines were there.

The other Vietnamese, with no sign of emotion, took her straw hat, covered her face, put her arms by her side, and mat-ter-of-factly turned back to finish working. They would take her to be buried when their work was done.

The Marines, confounded at the Vietnamese casual attitude toward their comrade's sudden death, shook their heads in bewilderment and continued on their march.

Shit Bird, Bird Shit . . .

Oop and Mad Dog were in Da Nang again and had looked up some old buddies. They couldn't help but notice a scowling American walking outside the tent. He had a ruddy complexion, a pugnacious look about him, a parrot on each shoulder, and a submachine gun draped across his chest. He was certainly a "fierce-looking warrior."

But to Oop and Mad Dog's eye he was just too pressed-out, too clean. Oop asked one of his friends, "What's the story on the parrot man?"

Oop's buddy laughed and said, "The guy has a complex. He had every one around here fooled for a long time. He looks for new men of lower rank that he can intimidate. He tells great sto-ries and calls everyone straight legs, or legs." (Legs means that they're not jump qualified.) But he fails to note that he's not jump qualified himself. At any rate he's never seen a shot fired in anger. He's stationed here in Da Nang. He does something for the headquarters people of the outfit that Rofsky's with, but they're so super secret we actually don't know what they do."

Mad Dog, being the ornery son of a bitch that he was, and not liking the braggart, went out and walked toward the bird man. The bird man, noting a new face in "his area" stiffened up and started strutting his stuff. Mad Dog could barely keep from breaking out in laughter. He walked by him and turned around.

"Hey buddy," he called.

The bird man turned around quickly, held on to his submachine gun and grimaced through properly-clenched teeth, "I'm not your buddy. I'm a Marine!"

"Well there, Marine, both your birds shit down your back!" Mad Dog broke out laughing, as did the men in the tent the Mad Dog had just left . . . thus leaving the shit bird with bird shit running down his back!

Trash . . .

One experience in Vietnam not to be missed was the trash dump run at headquarters. What the Americans wasted in a day could provide for a village for a week. When the Americans pulled up with their loads of trash, literally hundreds of Vietnamese descended on them, running like wild warriors to the dumping area. Crowds of Vietnamese would wait, and as the trucks approached they would wave for the Americans to dump where they were waiting. If the Americans went past a hundred yards or so, the people descended on them like they were giving out gold.

One thing that was learned early was that the Americans couldn't throw away batteries or anything that could be turned around and used against them. The Vietnamese would take the batteries, even the little flashlight batteries, and somehow recharge them, and then use them to detonate booby traps against the Americans. Some of the men actually got terrified of the Vietnamese. There were all ages, all types and no way to predict what they were really up to.

In one particular area where the Americans liked to go to dump trash, there was a Vietnamese woman, probably in her late twenties or early thirties, who had huge breasts. They would drive past whatever crowd she was in just to see her run up with her knockers flopping almost completely over her shoulders. Every guy tried to offer her something to go to bed with her. Eventually it was found out that she was a Viet Cong agent. She was killed while throwing grappling hooks in the retrieval of V.C. bodies.

So the Americans, as usual, were foolish, and their heads were turned by kids and women and tits.

Drafting, Viet Cong Style . . .

Vietnam has been in war, basically, for centuries. Some of the people grew up while their country was fighting the Japanese, others fighting the French, or whomever, and they were totally sick of war.

The V.C. would attempt to force-recruit farmers. They would come in and just take their children. Some of the farmers were so sick of war they refused to have anything to do with the Viet Cong. To set an example, the North Vietnamese or V.C., whoever happened to be operating in the area, would move into an area, gather the farmers who had tried to ignore them, kneel them down in front of the whole village, put a large caliber pistol to the back of their heads and shoot them. Their faces would disintegrate in blood and gore. (For those who don't know anything about weapons, a bullet makes a much bigger hole when it exits than when it enters.) This was done to hundreds upon hundreds of people who just wanted to be left alone. The Communists had a use for them, though. This was one of the ways they handled "draft" resistors.

Another thing that the Communists liked to do was to stake out these people, either lying down or standing up so that their legs and arms were spread apart. If they were standing up, this was done on two poles. After they tortured them and let them suffer for awhile, they would gather the whole village and disembowel them in front of everybody and just let them die in front of their families. This was a very convincing argument to help the little yellow bastards.

Care Packages . . .

Care packages to the men in the field were normally a joke. These were boxes approximately eighteen inches square that were packed with "goodies" . . . razors, chocolates, cigarettes. Our government, instead of replenishing things, used some of the C-rations left over from the Second World War. Normally the care packages that the field men received had been opened and raided by some schmuck in headquarters who took what he wanted (or they wanted) before passing them on to the troops. They would rifle the boxes, then send the men in the field the boxes with the garbage that they didn't want.

Mad Dog never would take any of them. He liked a good cigar occasionally, but he didn't like the cardboard ones that showed up in these "care" packages.

One day the men got some that hadn't been opened, which was a miracle in itself. One guy, when he opened his box, exclaimed, "What the hell is this?" and he held up a package of Lucky Strike cigarettes in a green package. The modern packaging was a red target bull's eye.

Oop immediately said, "That's a keepsake. I wouldn't open it."

The guy said, "Well, I have to try it. This is pre-Second World War."

He lit a match and put it to the cigarette and took a gigantic inhale for his first drag. The cigarette burned down like a fuse, and before he could react it actually burnt his lip. The men went totally hysterical with laughter.

Every green pack found after that was hopefully sent home, although most men know that a lot of packages that they mailed were also pilfered by the people working in the post offices. Mad Dog himself had sent a friend some tiger's eye cuff links and tie tacks and rings all matching and the box arrived at his friend's home completely empty. This wasn't an uncommon thing.

Chow . . .

The Army, which had newer and supposedly better equipment than the Marine Corps, had sent men to several different

outfits to find out why the Marine Corps was getting better classified information than they were. One man was sent to Rofsky
at Da Nang. There is a popular misconception among the men in
the services that the other service always has better chow. In
actuality, the Army, Navy and Marine's chow was basically the
same, but the Air Force definitely had the advantage when it
came to grub.

After the two men introduced themselves, the Army man
said, "I didn't get any breakfast. Can you get take me to the
chow hall?"

Rofsky said, "Sure. Come on."

They arrived at the chow hall and as they headed in, the Army
guy said, "I've been waiting for some of this good Marine Corps
chow!"

He stepped into the hall and stopped cold in his tracks. Laid
out before him was the same thing that the Army had! He turned
to Rofsky and quipped, "I thought you guys ate good. You eat like
us! Chicken wings for breakfast, chicken thighs and drum sticks
for lunch and chicken breasts for dinner!" They both laughed as
they started through the chow line to grease up, as they called
it.

Rest Assured . . .

Rofsky was sent to Marble Mountain to set up day and night
listening posts. It never occurred to him that he had not seen
any infantry men up there. When night came, actually when dusk
came, men started moving out with rifles. Some of them looked
oddly familiar. Rofsky went over to show them where his men
were and to find out where they would be digging in.

He discovered that the men guarding him at night were cooks
and band members that had been sent up from the band and
mess halls in Da Nang!

He thought to himself, "I guess it's true that every Marine is
a basic rifleman!"

Chopper Rescue . . .

During one of Mad Dog's reprieves from combat, he
scrounged up helicopter rides and just flew around to check out

different areas. One day they were to fly over an area where a recon patrol had been ambushed and killed. The grunt company went in and recovered the bodies and held the position until choppers came to remove the dead Marines. Mad Dog hitched a ride on one of the helicopters. The first chopper landed and the men loaded three of the dead Marines on it. As they took off, the second chopper moved in to get the last of the men who were killed.

Mad Dog and the machine gunner stood on either side of the doorway of the chopper. They grabbed the body bags as the four men on the ground, one on each side of the back of the body bag, and one on each side of the front pushed them up to them. Four Marines came running with a body and hoisted it up. Just as they bent and reached out for it, small arms fire erupted and the Marine's face disintegrated in front of Mad Dog's chest, splattering blood and gore all over his face and chest. The wounded Marine's body keeled from the impact, but Mad Dog, already in motion, grabbed him and hoisted him on board. If the Marine hadn't been running, the bullet would have hit Mad Dog directly in the chest. Mad Dog's eyes and the gunner's met for an instant, but there was no time to recognize the horror. Another man who had been hit in the small arms fire was hoisted to the door and they dragged him aboard as the chopper was taking off.

They tried to lay him down, but he fought to sit up. He started gurgling and choking. Mad Dog didn't know what to do. The gunner ran and told the pilot what was happening. A corpsman on the ground said, "Give him a trach."

They weren't sure what to do, so they snapped the headset onto Mad Dog and Mad Dog, following the corpsman's instructions, made a small incision into the man's throat, grabbed a ball point pen and jammed it into the trach tube and the man started breathing properly. This ballpoint pen tracheotomy saved a man's life.

Dog Patch . . .

Every major base had a dog patch—a little town of ramshackle huts and what have you—thrown up outside the gate by the Vietnamese. These were always full of bars, whorehouses, and "souvenir shops." (Most of the "souvenirs" that the guys got they didn't want to take home. They had to take those "souvenirs" to the field hospital and get penicillin shots for them. Penicillin didn't even cure some of the nameless crud they picked up over there.)

There were two young girls who had a little shop of what they called souvenirs, but which was really junk. The guys frequented the shop because the older of the two girls took them in back and screwed them for money. The younger girl was very hostile.

One day Mad Dog and Oop walked through the town to check it out. On their way back they went into this shop and saw both girls. They both concluded that the younger one was a V.C. agent and couldn't control her hatred of the Americans. Mad Dog and Oop told the M.P.s who were supposedly patrolling the village to check her out. They were laughed at. (There is little doubt the M.P.s were screwing the oldest girl themselves, and at a discount price because they were M.P.s and were letting the girls operate.)

A few weeks later some fire erupted along the edge of an area where Rofsky's company's equipment was and they found both girls, along with four men, dead. They were shot trying to creep through the wire to booby-trap the surveillance equipment.

Praying . . .

Mad Dog was not a religious man but he was not one to razz others about their beliefs. He also was never one to call men or women in other branches of military service belittling names. He once told some of his troops, "Never make fun of a man because of what service he chose."

JAPAN

Mad Dog did not want to take R and R but the captain and Oop talked him into it, finally saying that he would be ordered to go anyway. Mad Dog got Japan. He really didn't pick; he just took what was given to him.

The ride in the civilian airplane was smooth. Shortly after the meal was served—it was almost inhaled by the men on board—the all-female flight attendant crew quickly cleaned up. Mad Dog fell asleep, oblivious to the chatter of the men around him.

The men on board the aircraft were dressed in their "utilities" and although Mad Dog's had been washed, holes and blood stains were very evident. One of the officers on board made an announcement that the men would have to rent or buy civilian clothing at the base where they would be landing.

The plane landed and the men disembarked and headed for the clothing store. There was much hubbub while they rifled through the racks of clothing for rent. Mad Dog wisely asked where the PX was and made his way quickly there. He picked out three sets of "civvies" and six packs of "skivvies" (underwear) and was on his way he wasn't exactly sure where.

He had heard that Yokohama had a bay and a lot of ships. Mad Dog loved the ocean, more exactly the shore. Something about water seemed to calm and rejuvenate him. He walked quickly to the gate of the base where the waiting taxicabs were lined up. Several of the men who had gotten clothes quickly were there already and one shouted from a cab.

"Hey, buddy, want to share a ride?"

"Where ya headed?" Mad Dog asked.

"The Ginza," the voice from the cab answered.

"Go ahead," Mad Dog said, "I'm headed for Yokohama."

"Okay. See ya!" the voice yelled as the driver took off in a squeal of tires.

A cab pulled up. Mad Dog got in and said, "Yokohama."

The driver said, "Chinatown?" Chinatown was one of the bar districts.

Mad Dog said, "No, the harbor."

The driver questioned, "Harbor?" Not being able to say the "r," it came out "Hahboh?"

Mad Dog said, "Ships. Water." Then, almost as an afterthought, "A nice hotel."

The driver said, "You stay Ahh and Ahh?" meaning R and R.

Mad Dog replied, "Yes."

The driver said, "I take you number one hotel."

Mad Dog said, "Good deal."

The driver made small talk on the trip. Mad Dog had difficulty understanding him but they managed to communicate. The driver pulled to a hotel that occupied a corner of two streets. When Mad Dog got out he was surprised to see huge oceangoing vessels docked less than a quarter mile away. A street and park separated Mad Dog from the water. The cab driver had made a perfect selection.

Mad Dog checked in, asked for a room looking at the water and was taken to his room. He opened the drapes to look out across the park at the big ships. The hotel was at the extreme end of the park which extended for about a mile to his right.

Mad Dog brushed his teeth, shaved, and took a shower. Then he got into the Japanese tub, relaxing, quietly awed by the stillness and almost overcome by what may have been loneliness. He got dressed, ordered a bottle of gin, fresh limes, tonic and ice to be brought to his room. He told them he'd be back later to sign the guest check.

Mad Dog left the hotel and walked across to the park. He just stood and watched the ships for awhile and then started walking toward the *Hikawa Maru*, a ship docked permanently in the harbor and used as a tourist attraction. He had no intention of going on it but wanted to walk along the water to relax.

When he was about three quarters of the way through the park, he heard cries of "Help! Help!" Mad Dog looked first to the water, then quickly to the section of the park where trees were growing. He instinctively started to run toward the voices. He saw two small Japanese young women huddled together, crying, and four drunken Americans surrounding them, grabbing at their clothes.

"What in the hell is going on here?" he yelled.

One of the Americans said, "Fuck off, asshole. This is none of your business."

In perfect English one of the young women pleaded, "Please help us. Please! We're not bar girls!"

Mad Dog said, "Let 'em go, you scum bags!"

The American who had been doing the talking said, "Let's get him!"

The four now faced Mad Dog as he backed against a tree, his only protection.

The Japanese girls ran away toward the street that ran parallel to the park.

Mad Dog went into "Combat Mode." When the girls were clear, he let out a scream that sent chills up the four attackers' spines. Mad Dog punched the closest one to him and spun him around to shove him into the other three attackers. Mad Dog deftly moved to the side of the three remaining and cut down the second with two quick punches to the face. The talker was next. Mad Dog moved into him like lightning and used his face for a punching bag. It erupted into crimson from above the eyes, to the nose and mouth.

The fourth character said, "I don't want no trouble, buddy!"

Mad Dog said, "I ain't your buddy, you fucking pig!"

One smash to the jaw sent this one down and the four were all on the ground in various stages of consciousness, bleeding from different wounds inflicted by Mad Dog. Mad Dog looked down at them, slowly going from a "killer attitude" to one of disgust for the four. This probably saved their lives.

Mad Dog said, "Take your shoes off."

One of the dazed drunks said, "Huh?"

Mad Dog walked to him, bent over, grabbed his foot, picked it up roughly and ripped his shoe off. The others quickly took their shoes off.

Mad Dog said, "Throw them here," pointing to the ground in front of him.

When the other seven shoes were in front of him, Mad Dog gathered up the shoes and walked to the harbor wall. He unceremoniously tossed them into the water.

One of the drunks, now imminently more sober, shouted, "We're going to report you to the M.P.s!"

Mad Dog started back toward them. The four got up and started walking as quickly as they could without any shoes away from him. And, as all defeated bullies seem to do, made threats of "we'll get you" and "you're dead meat" and various other tough guy statements. All, of course, being said while in full retreat!

Mad Dog stopped and in his mind tried to decide what to do . . . sit on a bench and relax, go to his room and get stinking drunk, get a bar whore and get laid. The options were few, but any were stress-reducing.

As he was coming out of his self-induced thoughts, two limousines pulled to a stop on the street running parallel to the park. Out jumped four Japanese men, two from each limo, and held open the door of one of the cars. From it emerged a very distinguished-looking Japanese male about sixty years of age.

The men looked first at Mad Dog, then at the four retreating attackers. One of the Japanese men walked to Mad Dog and said in perfect American English, "Did you help my sisters escape from those drunks?"

Mad Dog looked at him a second, taken slightly by surprise at the perfect English, then replied, "Yeah. Sorry that some of these guys are such schmucks!"

The Japanese man said, "Schmucks?"

Mad Dog said, "Yeah. You know . . . dicks, pricks, whatever . . . "

The Japanese smiled a genuine smile.

"My parents would like to thank you. Would you mind coming to the car?" Then he added, "What's your name?"

"Most people call me Mad Dog. My real name is 'Hey You.'"

They both started to laugh and walked to the cars.

Mad Dog said, "David Matthews."

The Japanese extended his hand and said, "Jimmy Whitney."

Mad Dog said, "You're shitting me, right?"

Jimmy replied, "No. My dad's half English. My mom's full Japanese. She is the only one in our house who doesn't speak English. We all went to American-speaking schools. Are you stationed here?"

"I'm on R and R from Vietnam."

They were at the cars. Jimmy walked to his father, bowed the little bow that the Japanese do, and spoke in Japanese. His father nodded and grunted. The other three men hissed between their teeth and said, "Honto?" which means "True?"

Jimmy's dad held out his hand and said, "Thank you, sir, for protecting my daughters. Jimmy says you are here on R and R."

Mad Dog said, "Please call me Mad Dog, Dog, or Dave, sir. Yes, I'm here from Vietnam."

"Then you must make our home your headquarters."

"Thank you, sir. But I've got a room at that hotel," pointing to the hotel he had left.

The latter said, "Nonsense! Save your money! Stay with us."

The back door of the other limo was opened and a Japanese woman about the age of the Papasan emerged, being helped out by two attendants. The father spoke to her, yet she never took her eyes off Mad Dog. When the father finished talking, Jimmy, the son, spoke to her. All of this was in Japanese. The mother said something to Jimmy. He turned to Mad Dog and said, "My mother wants to know your full name."

Mad Dog said, "I told you."

Jimmy replied, "She wants to know if Dave is your only name."

Mad Dog said, "My first name is Ivan, but I don't use it. I don't even tell anyone."

Jimmy turned toward his mother and said, "Ivan."

She smiled, bowed, and said, "Ibu-chan!"

Then she turned to the father and said something. The father turned to Mad Dog and said, "My wife insists that you stay with us. We'll get your things from the hotel and you will stay with us."

Mad Dog was too shocked to protest and asked, "What do I call you?"

The father repeated his question to the mother in Japanese. She softly said, "Mamasan."

The father looked at Mad Dog. "That makes me Papasan. Let's go."

Mad Dog started to get into the car with the men when Mamasan spoke in Japanese. Papasan said, "Mamasan wants you to ride with her and the girls."

Mad Dog walked back to the car with the girls (there were three daughters in the family) and Mamasan and got in. The trip was lively as the girls chattered incessantly both in English and in Japanese. They thought Mad Dog was gorgeous, and he was their hero. Mamasan just smiled. She spoke to him in Japanese as though he understood . . . which he didn't.

The girls were constantly interpreting for him, and her, but it soon seemed unnecessary, as the mamasan and Mad Dog quickly seemed to understand each other even though neither spoke the other's language.

The home was beautiful, set on a hill but secluded by the landscaping. Actually on a small man-made plateau, the driveway wrapped around the hill and ended at the main house. Mad Dog was somewhat uncomfortable, as he was not used to such opulence.

His belongings were taken to the guest house. When this was announced, Mamasan quite untraditionally said, "Bring his belongings to our extra bedroom. He will sleep under our roof as our son."

Everyone was shocked at her statement. Yet there was no objection from anyone. Although a surprise, it seemed "right" to everyone. The family was excited by the prospect of showing the "real Japan" to a foreigner, since most servicemen only saw the bars and shopping streets, the "Ginza," "Isezaki Cho" and the various "Chinatowns."

Mad Dog was asked if he knew how to bathe Japanese style. He told them, "I know how to take a bath, but I don't know what you mean by Japanese style."

Jimmy explained. "The tub is used for soaking, after you clean. In traditional Japanese homes, you first dip the water out of the tub, wash, then dip to rinse. After you are washed and rinsed, you get into the tub." He then added, "We have a shower. So you can take a shower and then soak."

Mad Dog took this advice, and soaked in the hot water for a long time. He was almost asleep in the tub when Jimmy checked on him.

"We want to take you out to dinner. You like Japanese food?"

Mad Dog said, "It's okay. I'd just like to hit the sack. This bath took it out of me."

Jimmy, somewhat taken aback, said, "Okay." He went to tell the family.

Papasan said, "He must be tired from the trip here and needs to rest. Let's let him pick what he does. Maybe sleep and relaxing is the best for him."

Meanwhile, Mad Dog slowly dried and went to bed. He was asleep before his head was completely on the pillow. He slept the sleep of a contented, protected baby. For once it was a dreamless sleep . . . without the horror of war or the shame he felt for his childhood. He always managed to blame himself for the sadness and loneliness of his life. Oh, sweet sleep!

In the morning Mad Dog was in the state of half-sleep and half-awake, trying to remember where he was, when a light tap on the door brought him to reality.

"Ohayo guzi mus," came the voice of Mamasan from the other side of the door. Mad Dog presumed that this was "good morning" and answered, "Good morning. Be out in a minute."

He got out of bed, took a quick shower and went to the kitchen. Everyone was gathered for breakfast.

Papasan said, "We're going to eat an American breakfast today."

Mad Dog said, "I usually just have black coffee."

Papasan relayed this to Mamasan who was cooking while the maid watched her. Mamasan immediately said something in Japanese that everyone laughed at.

Jimmy spoke to Mad Dog. "Mama says you'll eat a good breakfast or you'll be spanked!" He added, "Our maid usually cooks, but Mamasan wanted to cook for you."

Mad Dog was instantly embarrassed and looked down. He had never had anyone do anything special for him, and did not know how to respond to compliments or caring except to be embarrassed and for some reason to feel guilty!

The maid, on orders from Mamasan, brought a pot of strong aromatic coffee to the table. After she sat it down she poured Mad Dog a cup and asked the others if they wanted any. Papasan and Jimmy had some, but the other children refused.

Mamasan called to the maid, who was already coming to her. Mama handed her a plate of steaks and picked up a serving platter full of fried eggs and brought them to the table. She started loading Mad Dog's plate. He tried to protest, but was ignored. Mama then put the platter down and went to the counter where she had sliced a beautiful, ripe red tomato. She proudly brought it back to Mad Dog and said in Japanese, "This is for you, Ibu-chan."

Papa repeated in English and Mad Dog humbly, almost in a whisper, said, "Thank you, Mama."

The entire family was beaming as the food was served, and all were excited about having Mad Dog as a guest.

Papa asked him, "When do you go back?"

"In three more days," was the reply.

Raiko, one of the daughters said, "I didn't know Americans could be bashful. They are always making obscene remarks to Japanese women. You're nice!"

The girls beside her pushed her shoulder and said in unison, "We think you nice, too!"

Jimmy and Papa began to laugh, and Mama asked what they said. When she was told, she looked down slightly and covered her mouth with her hand and laughed also.

It was a strange metamorphosis. The girls, who a day before would be ashamed, and in fact, not be caught dead with an

American, now wanted to show Mad Dog off to their friends. The chatter among the girls was of what they wanted to show Mad Dog, who was now "Ibusan" to them. Although they could say Ivan perfectly, "Ibu" was cuter.

They took him to Kyoto to see the temples, then in the afternoon to Tokyo to see the Imperial Palace and various shrines and gardens. In the evening they took him to the Ginza, the shopping street in Tokyo that was like none other in the world. Mad Dog stood out like a sore thumb in most places because foreigners were rare. But on the Ginza, Americans and other nationalities were seen with more frequency.

Everyone but Mad Dog was tired on the trip home. He was oddly comfortable with this family, and wondered why.

The next day, Mad Dog was again awakened by a gentle tapping on his door. He answered, took a quick shower and went into the kitchen to the greetings of the entire family.

They announced that Mamasan wanted to take a trip to an orphanage where they tried to go at least once a week. There they would take some of the children out to various activities like zoos, sightseeing, etc. Mad Dog wasn't quite sure he wanted to do this, but didn't want to offend anyone.

After breakfast Mamasan, Mad Dog and two of the girls got into the car and went to the orphanage. Upon arrival they were greeted warmly. Mad Dog was stared at. Several of the children walked by and said, "Hello." This was the only English they knew. Mamasan spoke briefly with the ladies in charge.

Two young boys, approximately five and six, were tearing around, making noise, yelling and screaming. They had to be corrected several times. Mad Dog instantly knew that if they were going to take children out, he would take these two.

He found out from one of the daughters that the boys were brothers. When Mamasan spoke to the girls, they told her that Mad Dog wanted to take the Oba brothers. She smiled. The workers at the orphanage giggled and put their hands over their mouths as was customary in Japan at the time.

Each of the girls took a child, Mama took a child, and Mad Dog with his two made four adults and five children. The boys ignored the fact that they had been told several times that Mad

Dog could not speak Japanese, and sat on each knee chattering away at him.

The day was full and happy. They went sightseeing to the Imperial Palace seeing several shrines throughout. They took the boys and girls to a nice lunch. The children weren't used to such fine food, and ordered more than they could eat. They stuffed themselves almost to the point of becoming ill. They were very, very happy.

The boys fell asleep in Mad Dog's arms on the trip back to the orphanage.

The next night the girls asked Mad Dog if he would like to go out somewhere. Mad Dog said, "Where do you suggest?"

They conferred together, and Raiko said, "We don't want to go to an American place."

Mad Dog said, "Well, what do you want to do?"

She put her hand over her mouth as she smiled and said, "There's a Greek restaurant called the Bacchanal where we see them dancing sometimes. Do you want to go there?"

Mad Dog said, "Sure. Let's go."

They arrived at the Bacchanal and went inside. They were greeted by the owner, a handsome Greek man and his wife, a stunningly beautiful, raven-haired woman who turned out to be an American. They introduced themselves (the owner's name was George and his wife was Lynn) and the girls introduced themselves and Mad Dog.

A great evening was had . . . wonderful Greek food, Lynn doing a spectacular belly dance with lit candles, and George teaching Mad Dog and the girls Greek folk dances . . . a giggling, happy time.

The days were a whirlwind for everyone. The family couldn't do enough for Mad Dog. His idea of being drunk for four days never materialized. In fact, the few beers with Papasan and at the Greek restaurant was the extent to which Mad Dog drank at all.

They insisted on taking him to the air base to catch his plane back to Vietnam. Raiko, the oldest of the girls, told Mad Dog when she hugged him goodbye, "Please write. And come back. We love you."

Then she added softly, "I love you." She cried and held on to him, starting to sob uncontrollably. Jimmy intervened and took her to the car.

Mad Dog shook hands with Papasan and thanked him for everything.

Jimmy was back, and shook hands. He said, "Dave, please stay in touch. If you can, come back."

Mamasan looked through tear-filled eyes, bowed properly, and then as though taken over by an unseen force, stood straight and took the few steps to Mad Dog and hugged him, saying in Japanese, "You are my son. Come back."

She was assisted away by Papasan and young Jimmy.

Mad Dog picked up his bag, turned, and was through the gate of the air base. He walked quickly, turned once, waved, and then disappeared into the night.

THE RETURN

The men were totally subdued on the plane ride back to Vietnam. Most were extremely hung over, some were still drunk and a few even sick from drinking too much. When the meal was served, Mad Dog refused politely and tried to relax, keeping his eyes closed so that he wouldn't have to talk to anyone. He was on his way home to combat. Yet for the first time in his life he had a sad, weary feeling caused by leaving someone he truly loved.

The plane landed at Da Nang. As the men were leaving the plane, automatic weapons were heard inside the huge building where the new group of men going on R and R were waiting for the plane. One of the officers off the plane first opened the door where the shots were coming from and was hit squarely in the forehead with a bullet, killing him instantly. Men started looking for cover anywhere they could find to hide. They were, naturally, all unarmed.

Mad Dog ran to the side of the building, looked through the window, and saw three Viet Cong taking turns firing at the unarmed Americans who were trying to hide. Fortunately there were some heavy pew-like seats that offered protection. Mad Dog had a few followers. He said, "Let's go in the front door and hit them from behind."

The small group followed Mad Dog and they slowly opened a door that went to the head (bathrooms). The inside door to the main waiting area had been removed and Mad Dog peered out to see the Viet Cong not ten feet away with their backs to him. Mad Dog didn't say a word, just motioned the others with him.

Mad Dog led the charge, knocking two of the Viet Cong down. The others charged past him and disabled the third. The Marines pounced on and disarmed the Viet Cong and were frisking them when a group of A.P. (Air Police) came bursting in, after peeking through the door and seeing the Marines manhandling the Viet Cong.

A captain said, "Back off, Marines. We'll take charge."

Mad Dog looked at the officer and said, "Where the fucking hell were you? They could have killed everyone here!"

The captain said, "You better watch it, Marine!"

Mad Dog looked him in the eye and said one word, "Asshole!"

The Air Police took the prisoners away and Mad Dog later was informed that the entire squad of A.P.s were given Bronze Stars and the captain a Silver Star. Mad Dog and the others got nothing.

R AND R, HAWAII

Oop's R and R was to Hawaii. He really looked forward to meeting his wife. There had never been anyone else for these two. Patty had been Oop's high school sweetheart. She was slightly on the thin side, but was by no means skinny. She had a regal look to her that came naturally. The other wives seemed to be drawn to her for solace. When one of the husbands was lost or wounded, she was always among the first to offer help to the widow or wife.

They had two beautiful children, both girls, Lisa and Shirley.

They were at the airport when Oop's plane landed. The girls shrieked and jumped up and down yelling, "Daddy! Daddy!"

Patty, controlling herself, took only a few halting steps toward the gate where Oop would pass through. The girls were all over him, and he carried one on each arm, even though Lisa was a little too old for this in some people's mind.

He got to Patty and it seemed that the world got quiet. He put the girls down. Oop and Patty embraced and kissed, forever, it seemed. The love had never left these two. If anything, it grew. And it showed.

When the embrace ended, Patty said, "I have a sitter for the girls so we can be together."

Oop smiled and said, "Let's go."

They made the trip in their station wagon, driven by another Marine wife whose husband was stationed in Hawaii. She dropped Oop and Patty off and told the girls that she would be taking them for that afternoon and evening. The girls protested mildly, but suddenly seemed to understand, started giggling and said okay.

The reunion was more than either hoped for.

Oop said, "I may have forgotten how."

Patty said, "We'll retrain together, Marine."

They loved each other with a sweet and gentle, yet passionate love that thrilled them both all over again.

The next day the whole family went shopping and to the beach. Oop and Patty slipped away for a few hours, as their friend Donna came back to take the girls to lunch.

The same love and respect and admiration Oop and Patty had for each other was still there, as strong as ever. That special feeling between them was something that others saw and felt and in most cases wanted in their marriage and relationship. Those who knew them even a little, felt the marriage was truly made in Heaven.

The stay, as always, was too short. Patty took Oop to the airport alone. He had said his goodbyes to the girls and never mentioned anything negative as so many did, dwelling on, "If anything happens, you take care of Mommy, etc., etc." Oop felt the kids didn't need to wonder what could happen. He wanted the kids to be kids and enjoy childhood.

Some wives were hysterical at the airport. Some men who had been picked up by wives were now alone, getting their "Dear John" in person. Some of the wives actually wanted to introduce their new love to the old.

Patty and Oop talked quietly. He told her that he'd forgotten to tell her, but Mad Dog may be coming through Hawaii and he'd told him to stop off to try to see her.

He said, "He's a good young Marine. He reminds me of me in my younger, crazier days."

They both laughed and held each other.

As the last call was made for the men to board the plane, Oop looked at Patty and said, "I love you."

Patty said, "I know. I've always loved you."

They kissed and hugged each other, eyes closed, to memorize the sweetness of the moment.

Oop turned and was gone.

R AND R, PE NANG

Willie Miter and John Nebson were trying to decide where to go on R and R. Several men had just returned from R and R in Pe Nang.

"How'd it go," Willie asked. "How was Pe Nang? And where the hell is it?"

"It's in Malaysia," one of the men replied. "Man, you wouldn't believe it. Cheap booze, cheap hotels, cheap women, cheap everything! One thing you gotta see is this dame, 'Jenny Rose.'"

"Oh, yeah, why?"

"I ain't gonna tell you, but have a couple of drinks before you go," he said laughing. "You ain't gonna believe it!"

This was enough for Willie and John. They signed up with several others for Pe Nang.

There is a certain mystery about combat mentality. It makes a brotherhood that might otherwise never happen. Regardless of the stories of Black hating White, Hispanics hating these and Orientals hating those, it's not true. In combat, a man doesn't worry about the color of his comrade, or care. All they ever care about is protecting each other. It really can't be described or written about, but everybody who's been in combat feels it. So when one guy gets a totally outrageous scheme, it's like a snow-ball or wildfire. It seems to spread and grow and although every one knows that it is insane, impossible and makes absolutely no sense, no one will try to stop it. What follows is that kind of story.

The meal on the plane was their first non-C-ration meal since they arrived in Vietnam. It was steak, and the men ate slowly, savoring each bite. They talked about what they would like to do ... screw the stewardess' brains out, etc., etc., talking about how much they could drink when most of them hadn't had more than three drinks in their life, etc.

Most of the men got to their hotels and took a shower, met at the bar and started roaming the town. A few stayed in their room to drink and just enjoy the ice. Some of the men had almost actually forgotten what ice was—just frozen water. They hadn't seen it for months.

A group of bar-hopping moose hunters, also known as pussy patrols, stopped by a street cart for a sandwich. (People are always amazed that the first place guys coming from overseas want to go is a hamburger joint. When you don't have a hamburger for a long time, it's like steak and lobster to the rest of us.) The meat was different, but everything was. They saw an outdoor pen full of dogs.

One Marine said, "Let's take a dog back. He'll warn us when we're on patrol." When you're drunk, anything or nothing makes sense.

They called the man tending the dogs and picked out a shepherd-looking dog.

The old man said, "Come back one hour."

The Marine paid and said, "Maybe longer, but you no sell to nobody." It's funny how we think if we speak pidgin English everybody else understands us. Anyway, the old man nodded, understanding, and smiled happily.

Miter and Nebson stepped up, and Miter asked in pidgin English, "You know Jenny Rose?"

The old man said, "Ahhh, Jenny Rose," smiling and nodding his head.

With that the old man hailed a taxi, spoke to the driver, looked at the Marines and said, "You go."

The two Marines got into the cab and were off on their Jenny Rose adventure. They were greeted by an elderly lady at the door of the apartment they were taken to. She motioned to a seat and at the same time said, "Beer?"

Both men said, "Yeah."

The old lady disappeared for a few minutes and came back with two small glasses of beer. A TV was playing in the room that the two Marines were seated in, but the Marines did not understand one word of what was being said.

The old lady asked, "Who go first?"

Miter, the drunker of the two, jumped up and said, "Me!"

He entered the room that the old lady led him to and saw an average-looking woman of what he guessed to be about thirty with nothing on but a thin smock type top.

She said, "Undress and sit on the bed."

He quickly undressed and sat, slightly embarrassed even in his inebriated state, on the edge of the bed. Jenny Rose got a pan of water, washed and rinsed his privates, then dried them, doing what she thought was an erotic massage and said, "Lay down."

The by-now nervous young Marine, laid down.

Jenny Rose said, "You stay Army or Marine?"

Miter said, "Marine."

She said, "Okay."

She slithered down his body, took his manhood in her mouth, and began to hum the "Marine Corps Hymn."

Miter broke out in gales of uncontrollable laughter while Jenny Rose hummed, "From the Halls of Montezuma," etc., etc., etc.

Meanwhile, the other men drank and screwed and had started back to the hotel when they remembered the dog. They had the cabby take them to the place where the dogs were. When the Marine who paid for the dog asked the old man where his dog was, the old man said, "Inside," and pointed to the building next door that had a store front.

The Marines walked over, and again he asked for his dog. The old man said something to the man behind the counter and the shopkeeper started putting packages on the counter.

The Marine protested, "No, no. I buy a dog."

The man behind the counter said, "Yes, this your dog."

The Marine suddenly got ill. The dogs were for sale to eat. He was then informed that the sandwich they had eaten was also dog meat. The Marine staggered outside and upchucked all of the food and booze of the day. Pe Nang was a place they would never forget!

NIGHT LANDING

One day while Mad Dog was at Chu Lai, he and Sergeant Rofsky were relaxing and shooting the breeze. Rofsky said, "The brass in their infinite wisdom are going to attempt a night landing. But the scuttlebutt that I get is that no one will volunteer to drive the first jeep."

"You're shitting me! There's always a bunch of gung ho Gyrenes who will volunteer to do anything. "

Just then Oop approached and said, "What are you two concocting?"

Mad Dog and Rofsky chuckled, as did Oop. Mad Dog answered, "Word has it that no one will volunteer to drive the first jeep on the night landing."

Oop replied, "It's not lack of volunteers, it's lack of volunteers with a high enough clearance."

"Do I have a high enough clearance?" Mad Dog asked.

"Yeah, you do."

Mad Dog laughingly said, "I'll volunteer."

"I knew you would. That's why I came to talk to you."

Oop and Mad Dog walked back to the command post together, and Oop addressed the C.O. "Mad Dog has volunteered to take the first piece of equipment in on the night landing. He has the proper clearance for this."

"Fine," replied the C.O. "I'll have radio contact made with the ship. It's already on its way from Da Nang."

The C.O. said to Mad Dog, "Get your gear. All you'll need is your rifle, some ammo and your canteens."

"Yes, sir," said Mad Dog as he and Oop turned to leave. Oop drove Mad Dog to the helicopter pad. Mad Dog boarded and was taken to the ship.

En route the crew chief of the chopper informed Mad Dog, "There ain't no landing pad on this ship, so we're going to winch your ass down."

"Those sons of bitches," Mad Dog said aloud, "No one told me this shit!"

The crew chief answered, "Your people probably didn't know, but the big brass sure as hell did!"

"It figures," snorted Mad Dog.

When they reached the ship, Mad Dog was attached by a cable to the harness the crew chief had fitted him in and winched down to the ship. As he was being lowered Mad Dog said a few oaths and questioned the legitimacy of the birth of whoever had dreamed this up. However, he wasn't hurt and he boarded the ship safely.

A lieutenant colonel and a major quickly approached him. They introduced themselves and told Mad Dog to follow them, which he did. Mad Dog wasn't familiar with the different rooms on naval vessels. He presumed they had arrived at some sort of conference room. There were several Marine officers and several Navy officers waiting.

Each one briefed him separately, making Mad Dog think that they each thought their part of the operation was the most important one, and that they were beating their chest for the senior Naval and Marine Corps officers there.

"I don't know what the hell the big deal is," Mad Dog thought to himself. "It looks like just another night landing to me. These chicken shit Navy and Marine Corps brass that thought this up just want to give themselves some chicken shit medal for their initiative and great planning skills. What the hell! Navy Seals are to swim in, put in markers, and then I'm to take the jeep and classified equipment in. And for some unknown reason an empty cargo trailer! That don't seem like no extraordinary operation to me. Bunch of assholes is all."

The talking went on and on.

"This is boring as hell," he thought as he yawned. "When the hell do I get away from these shit heads?"

Finally the briefing was over and they told him someone would take him to a rack if he wanted to rest, or he could eat. Mad Dog, who hadn't eaten that day said, "I'll try some of this Navy chow."

An enlisted sailor was called and took Mad Dog to the Navy mess hall. As they were walking, the sailor said, "This is so secret everyone on the ship knows what's going on. Why in the hell are they sending you in by yourself? The landing craft was designed to take men or equipment. Why don't they land a company of Marines first, and then send in the equipment? Why are they sending in one piece of equipment first?"

Mad Dog looked at him and said, "You know, I never knew sailors very good. You seem like a regular guy. Apparently you haven't been in the service long enough. These guys could fuck up a wet dream! If you don't know that by now, you better learn it!"

The sailor laughed. When he repeated the story, Mad Dog's stock went up all over the ship. The men thought that some vicious, gung ho, half insane person had come aboard, which Mad Dog normally was, but when the humor of his comment was spread, the men lightened up and were friendly to him.

The landing wasn't supposed to take place until 0200. Mad Dog racked out, but as soon as the sun began to go down, he was sent for. Again some insignificant junior Naval officer explained in great detail how the ship's outer doors open, the compartment was flooded, and the landing craft driven off. Mad Dog really didn't give a shit and everyone who looked at the officer lecturing Mad Dog knew that Mad Dog was bored as hell. But the officer kept right on rattling along.

Mad Dog thought to himself, "Wonder why this guy don't just shut up. I ain't never gonna see another one of these ships, let alone be on one to make another night landing. I really don't give a shit what the functions of the ship are. I'm just riding in it. I don't intend to captain one!"

The lecture went on for several minutes, but it seemed to Mad Dog like several hours. When this young officer was done, the Marine Corps officers stood, watching the loading of the equipment, and Mad Dog sauntered away. He began talking to some of the Marines and enlisted sailors. None of them could figure out why Mad Dog was being sent in by himself when they could send a company of Marines or more, or they could have Marines march overland to protect the area.

It was decided that the Navy just wanted to make a night landing. They could say they did it to practice. No one could figure out why classified equipment was being sent in except that the brass wanted it to look like it was a secret. But everyone aboard the ship knew what was going on.

Mad Dog thought to himself, "I wouldn't be surprised if half of Vietnam knows!"

Finally the time came. Mad Dog went down and got in the landing craft. He was told where to stand for his ride in. The big doors of the ship opened up. The area was flooded where the smaller landing craft was, and when there was enough water, it chugged out and headed for shore.

The landing thus far was very uneventful. The water and sky were all dark. One of the sailors on board pointed out to Mad Dog the lights that had been installed as markers. They were very dim and could only be seen from the seaward side. They chugged between them, and went ever so slowly, so as not to hit any unseen obstacles. Mad Dog couldn't help but wonder why they coasted in, since he was going to have to start up a jeep and drive it off, and jeeps were not exactly noted for their quietness.

He was told to get in the jeep. He got in. It was untied quickly and very efficiently by the sailors. They told him good luck. The front ramp of the landing craft fell forward. Mad Dog fired up the jeep, put on his night light, and drove off slowly and carefully. When he cleared he heard the motors of the landing craft start up, the ramp was lifted and the landing craft backed out.

Mad Dog drove slowly to where he was told that he was to rendezvous with the others. He drove to his appointed position, turned the jeep off and waited. Nothing was stirring, everything was quiet.

Finally Mad Dog got bored. He got out, walked around the jeep, and took a leak. He wondered what was going on, thinking, like all sergeants think, that he could run the operation better than the brass. And he was probably right.

At last he heard some noise and voices. He hurried back to the jeep, and took out his weapon, which he had set on full automatic. He walked toward where he heard the voices. The sound was clearer now, and the voices were definitely Americans talking.

Mad Dog decided to end his boredom and have some fun. To his left was a huge tree. He walked over and positioned himself behind it, out of range or view of the approaching Americans. He opened up, firing on full automatic into the ground.

There were screams and yelling. The Americans coming for the rendezvous didn't know exactly where the firing came from because Mad Dog, hidden behind the tree, had pointed his rifle at the ground so they couldn't see a flash and couldn't hear bullets going by. They started shooting wildly, bullets flying everywhere. The firing stopped; Mad Dog crept back to the jeep, and got in the seat. He put in a new loaded magazine into his weapon. When he spotted their approaching silhouettes, Mad Dog slouched down and pulled his hat over his eyes to look like he was sleeping.

The infantry company crept toward the rendezvous point at the landing spot. Mad Dog was still faking sleep. One guy spotted the jeep, and in shock at what he thought had happened, exclaimed, "Oh, my God! We've killed the guy we're supposed to be rendezvousing with!"

They rushed to the jeep. Mad Dog, lifting up his utility cover, said, "It's about time you fuckers got here! What was all the racket?"

Most of the men started laughing, but the officers and several of the senior N.C.O.s were pissed off, as usual.

Mad Dog laughed, then queried, "Where are we supposed to go?"

"We can't move out with this vehicle until daylight," was the reply.

This, then, made the insanity of the whole situation even more inane and stupid. The rest of the party did not land until daybreak even though Mad Dog's landing was uneventful.

Mad Dog approached the company commander. "Sir, requesting permission to go to sleep now."

By this time, the captain had regained his sense of humor. He suspected that Mad Dog was the one who had started the firing, and had commented that he didn't think that Mad Dog was beneath pulling a prank or two. "Permission granted to sleep, Sergeant."

Mad Dog crawled in the trailer and fell into a fitful sleep.

The next morning as the sun was coming up, the radios crackled to life. The landing was about to begin. When all the equipment and men went off the ship, the Marine company that had walked to meet Mad Dog the previous night was loaded on trucks and was to lead the small convoy of Marines with the classified equipment to where they were to report.

The going was very slow as they were not carrying any load and all the vehicles were in four-wheel drive. They finally hit an unpaved road and picked up speed, but soon came to a town and once again were ordered to slow down.

Mad Dog, in his jeep, was immediately behind the first truck that was full of Marines. As they slowed down through the village, they passed some children who were playing. The Americans began waving. Just then one of the children flipped a stick and a snake went flying through the air.

The Marines tried to duck, but it hit one and bit him on the neck. Another Marine killed the snake with his rifle. They immediately stopped and called a corpsman. He had no antivenom. They removed the Marine from the truck and called in a helicopter to take him. Mad Dog knew he would not live long enough to make it. By the time the helicopter arrived, the young Marine was in the throes of death.

The children were nowhere to be seen, and life seemed to be casually going on as normal for the rest of the village.

FENIG

The duty around Cam Lo was frustrating to some and relaxing to others. Men in their off-duty time got suntans, tried to get laid, listened to occasional bullshit from Fenig, cleaned their weapons, wrote letters home, and just relaxed. Fenig's presence had become almost as desired as V.D.

One night when Mad Dog's squad had the watch duty on the perimeter, Mad Dog noticed some movement in front of his positions. He sighted his rifle in on the movement and cranked off three quick shots. The object seemed to disappear. Mad Dog popped a hand flare to see what was going on. He couldn't see much, because the hand flares only last for about ten seconds. He radioed for a mortar flare and told the other squads on guard that he was going to investigate what, if anything, he had hit.

Mad Dog ran out with his men covering him. He found a cone-shaped rice straw hat with blood splattered on it. He returned to his position and he found Lieutenant Fenig there. Fenig, without asking, tore the hat from Mad Dog's hand and said, "Follow me."

The Dog's men looked at their sergeant, and he gave a look of, "I don't know what's going on."

The men shrugged, and off Mad Dog went to follow the lieutenant. Fenig headed straight to the command post to the battalion executive officer. Lieutenant Colonel Edwards happened to be on duty at the time. He was a mustang, a Marine who had come up through the ranks from private to lieutenant colonel. He bridled his contempt and dislike for Fenig because he did not want to impair his judgment.

Fenig, in a loud voice, said to Colonel Edwards, "Colonel, this man opened fire and probably killed an innocent civilian. He didn't say, 'toi' or 'dung lai' as I told the men to do."

The entire populace of the command post turned to look at this self-righteous idiot. Some of the staff N.C.O.s and officers had thought that Fenig was just gung ho and an excitable young lieutenant. Now even they looked at him with total wonder and amazement. Most of their jaws were dropped down and mouths open.

Mad Dog looked first at the lieutenant, then at Colonel Edwards, then back to Fenig. "Toi, your fuckin' ass, Lieutenant." He turned, looking straight at the lieutenant. "If some sneaky gook son of a bitch is in front of my position in the middle of the fucking night, I'm going to blow his ass off. And if anybody around me says anything in Vietnamese, I'm going to wax them too. You might not know it, sir, but this ain't Pendleton. Those little bastards are out to kill us, and I'd rather see a million dead gooks than one dead American!"

The lieutenant was taken aback. Snickering was beginning to be heard from some of the occupants of the command post. It was one of those ridiculous things in life that happen, and the way that Mad Dog presented his rebuttal really got things going.

The lieutenant drew himself up to full height and said, "Sergeant! What if that were me out there and you shot me?" Fenig had a half-smile, thinking he had really pulled a coup on Mad Dog.

Mad Dog didn't even blink an eye. "Lieutenant, if that were you out there, several things would have happened. First, every swinging dick in this fuckin' battalion would believe in God. Second, not only would I've had the whole shit pot of us empty our magazines, I'd a' called in fifty H.E.s and fifty Willie Peters. Then I'd a' pissed on your grave!"

The men in the command post could no longer hold it. Gales of riotous laughter broke out. They were actually leaning on each other, doubling over, some sat down, some fell to their knees so that they wouldn't drop over from laughing. Even Colonel Edwards had to turn his face away from looking at the sergeant, because every time he started to say something, he would laugh uncontrollably.

When there was a brief reprieve in the laughter, Mad Dog, who hadn't cracked a smile, said, "Any other dumb fuckin' questions, Lieutenant? I gotta get back to my post."

The last half of what he said was nearly drowned out, as his statement brought another outburst of crazy laughter from the Marines in the command post. Fenig was livid and trying to look ferocious. He had absolutely no effect on Mad Dog, who asked the colonel's permission to return to his post. The colonel just waved him out, afraid he might again break into gales of laughter if he tried to talk.

The next day when word got around of what had happened, the lieutenant couldn't go anywhere without some Marines saying, "*Toi! Dung lai!* Dung heap!" Fenig silently cursed Mad Dog and never accepted the fact that he was wrong and if the men would have listened to him and done what he wanted, they would have been giving their positions away making it easier for the N.V.A. to attack, overrun them or just lob grenades and shoot at them.

GRAPPLING HOOKS

One section of the Marines' area bordered a tree line. When night fell the men stationed in this area were always tense. They could occasionally hear animals moving around, and had to keep alert to be sure it was not enemy troops. Once a tiger wandered close to their position. The men were more interested in looking at it than shooting it and the animal ran back into the tree cover.

The North Vietnamese occasionally probed the American defenses with small groups of men, seemingly not really to do damage, but hoping to slip a few of the Communists inside the perimeter where they would be able to raise havoc and maybe assassinate the general. On one such probe, the Marines discovered why, when they were sure they had hit someone when they were firing, even though they would find blood, clothing and equipment, they would rarely find bodies.

The North Vietnamese crept out of the trees, and before they had gone twenty feet, the Marines opened fire on them. There were five N.V.A.s. They were cut down in their tracks. Seconds after, a flare from a mortar lit up the sky. The Marines saw one of the N.V.A.s move into the jungle flat to the ground, but he did not seem to be moving any of his appendages. The Marines opened fire on him, but he kept moving.

Then one of the men said, "They're pulling him in! I saw a rope."

Mad Dog said, "Spray the tree line."

The Marines opened fire into the tree line along where the N.V.A.s had come from and where the young P.F.C. said the rope entered the jungle. Oop came running on the double and Mad Dog said, "Gunny, let me take a couple of men and work along the tree line. They were pulling one of the gooks somehow. So I had our men pour some fire in the air where it came from."

Oop said, "Go ahead. I'll wait here. Be careful, but be quick."

Oop called Toth, Whipkey and Caputi. The three were up and following Mad Dog. Mad Dog was at a trot with the three behind him. He hit the tree line and started to where the N.V.A. had come out. When they got to within thirty feet, Mad Dog held up his hand to stop the three. He motioned for them to spread out, and ran to where the rope entered the tree cover. There he found three dead North Vietnamese women. They had ropes with grappling hooks attached still grasped in their hands.

When a man was hit, they would throw the hooks, impale the man, and pull him into the jungle so the Americans couldn't find the body. Thereby, if the Americans were truthful in their body count, they wouldn't have any.

Mad Dog checked to make sure the five N.V.A. were dead. Two were dead from the Marines' fire, two were still alive. The one with the grappling hook, also dead, had his hands around the hook. He apparently had been alive when the hook hit his chest. The three women pulled the rope and the grappling hook was pulled up and caught in his chin. As the women pulled the rope, the N.V.A. helplessly tried to pull the grappling hook out of his chin. It was a gruesome sight.

Mad Dog looked down and to no one in particular said, "Un-fuckin'-believable!"

Mad Dog motioned to his three men and said, "Get the women out here. Two of the N.V.A.s are alive. Caputi, get back and tell Oop. He can send two stretchers and have the mortar keep this place lit up for us."

Caputi said, "Rog, Dog," and was off directly toward the Marine perimeter where he had come from.

TOI DUNG LAI

One night when Mad Dog's squad was not on duty, he and his men were relaxing in a rear area. Sergeant Hampton, an inexperienced squad leader under Lieutenant Fenig's command, was on duty at the perimeter.

Lieutenant Fenig's greatest talent, it seemed, was in giving stupid orders. He thought, out of some ill-conceived idea, that if a Vietnamese showed up at camp and *said* they were not enemy, they were to be believed and treated with courtesy and offered all the protection the camp had to offer. He was so concerned about following the proper protocol to the letter, that he had issued orders to his men on guard at night, in this case specifically to Sergeant Hampton, that if they heard noises, they were to shout, *"Toi. Dung lai."* (This translates as two different ways of saying stop.) His purpose in this was to insure that no innocent civilians would be accidentally shot in the darkness. It would never occur to Lieutenant Fenig that no innocent civilians would be moving around the heavily guarded camp in the middle of the night.

To make matters even worse, *"Toi. Dung lai,"* was, in fact, incorrect Vietnamese, which would make it even more clear to any enemy within earshot that the person shouting it was an

American. He had, of course, completely refused to recognize the truth in Mad Dog's statements previously.

They had been on duty for several hours when one of Sergeant Hampton's men alerted him of some movement in his area. Stupidly and fatally he was obedient to Lieutenant Fenig's order and shouted, *"Toi. Dung lai,"* into the darkness. The reply to his call was answered by grenades and small arms fire from automatic weapons that sprayed the entire area. He had given the Marine position totally away.

The North Vietnamese had baited them. They moved men in front of the Marines, and when the Marines' attention was concentrated there, they attacked from the side and front annihilating the entire squad.

The noise of the automatic weapons and exploding grenades put everyone even in the rear areas on alert. The North Vietnamese poured through the gap that they had created. The Marines who were still alive were bayoneted as they lay wounded.

Oop screamed to his men. Mad Dog's men were already up. The North Vietnamese were on them. There was no time for fire fights—it was brutal hand-to-hand combat. The Marines stabbed and hacked, some using their bayonets, some using machetes, some using their issue K-bars to slash and fight away, all using whatever they could get their hands on.

The action was brutal and intense. The North Vietnamese and Marines locked in deadly struggles throughout. The North Vietnamese had wanted to get in to assassinate the general, and the Marines, by instinct and training, were not going to let this happen. They would die in their tracks trying to prevent it.

A North Vietnamese officer ran up and started to train his machine gun on the tents. Mad Dog was close, but in mortal combat with another Communist. He slashed his K-bar to the throat of his combatant, then quickly grabbed for the officer's automatic weapon.

The officer fired it as he grabbed, burning Mad Dog's hand. Mad Dog rammed his K-bar up and into the officer, raising him off his feet. As Mad Dog probed for his heart, the officer's hand went limp. Mad Dog ripped his K-bar out, letting the Communist drop to the ground to die.

Mad Dog turned the automatic weapon around and raked a group of Communists running toward the same area, killing them in their tracks. From the left side, his peripheral vision warned him. He ducked and raised his arm just as a North Vietnamese was trying to smash his face in with the butt of his rifle. The blow hit high on Mad Dog's arm and, being off balance, knocked him to the ground. The Communist turned his rifle around and was going to bayonet Mad Dog where he fell on the ground. Mad Dog threw his K-bar with all his might.

The blade entered the left eye of the Communist as Mad Dog rolled out of the way. The Communist staggered forward and impaled his bayonet in the ground where Mad Dog had been lying. Mad Dog was up, quickly rolled the North Vietnamese over, pulled his K-bar out and was on the attack again.

Oop, in the meantime, was almost immediately behind Mad Dog to form the final defense for the general's tent. Several of the Communists had broken through. Oop had an entrenching tool that he had sharpened on the tips and both sides while in Da Nang. He had it locked open and was swinging it like a scythe. As the North Vietnamese came in like demented maniacs, Oop showed why he was called Alley Oop. He swung his entrenching tool at the first, almost decapitating the Communist hell-bent on killing the general. The Communists almost seemed in a daze, trying to get to where the general had been sleeping.

Oop smashed the second in the face with his fist, and then kicked him hard to the side of the head. Now his entrenching tool was loose from the first one. He jerked it out and it went across his body, so when the third came, he backhanded it into the man's temple and face. The Communist went down, but he was still alive. Oop stepped on his hand so that he could not detonate the explosives that he was carrying. The Communist was tough and started to struggle.

Out of nowhere, Mad Dog came flying with his K-bar, ramming it into the Communist throat and ripping it out with blood flying everywhere. No words were exchanged as Mad Dog and

Oop continued to fight and kill to defend the general. The fight was long and hard. There was much carnage. The Marines had defended the general's position. The gap was closed. The eerie light of flares kept the area lit for protection. The North Vietnamese bodies were gathered into a pile. At first light the wounded Marines had already been carried to the field hospital there. The bodies of the dead were being tagged to be taken out and sent home.

Mad Dog put ointment from his medical kit on his hand where he had been burned when he had grabbed the barrel of the automatic weapon. His uniform was ripped; he was covered with blood, as were many of the other men. He couldn't tell if it was his blood or that of others. The men were bloody and filthy and tired, but they were relieved and grateful for the morning sun.

When the captain was making a tour to check on his men, he got the story of what had happened to Sergeant Hampton. Mad Dog got it from some of the men in a nearby squad who had heard Hampton yell *"toi,"* thereby exposing their position and making them vulnerable to the North Vietnamese attack. Mad Dog looked at Oop and said, "Oop, somebody better do something about that fucking Fenig, or he's going to get us all killed."

Oop said, "I think you're right, Dog. I better talk to the captain in private."

As Oop walked away to get his company commander, Mad Dog sat down on the ground. He grabbed his canteen, took a short sip, spit it out and dumped the remainder on his head.

THE CAPTURE

The C.O., Captain Wilson, wanted Mad Dog for a reconnaissance patrol. He called Dog in after his introductory meeting with his officers and staff N.C.O.s. The captain asked, "Sergeant Matthews, would you be interested in leading a small Snoop and Poop patrol? We are getting a lot of radio signals in this area but need visual sightings."

Mad Dog asked, "When do we move out?"

"Tonight." Almost as an afterthought the captain added, "Lieutenant Fenig has volunteered to be in charge."

Mad Dog's eyes lit up as he said, "Captain, this isn't exactly what I thought it would be. Maybe somebody else can do a better job."

"Nonsense," said the new C.O. "With Oop on R and R, everyone felt you should be the one to go."

Mad Dog blurted out, almost ashamed, "Sir, I thought lead meant to be in charge. If you order me, I'll go, but I got no respect for Lieutenant Fenig. He gets too many men killed for no reason."

Fenig jumped up and screamed in Mad Dog's face, "You better respect me and remember I'm an officer and you're an enlisted man!"

The captain said, "Do you respect the rank?"

Mad Dog replied, "Yes, sir."

Captain Wilson said, "That's all that is necessary. Besides, it's too late to change the plans now."

When the patrol gathered at the chopper path it included Fenig, Mad Dog, and three men that Mad Dog hardly knew. One, a black Marine, said to Mad Dog, "You don't know me too good. But Carl told me what you did. Man, you are a real fighting motherfucker! My name is Charles."

Mad Dog said, "Just doing my job," and added, "do you know these other guys?"

"Yeah," Charles said, "the radio man is a technical ace. He's not much in a fire fight but we ain't gonna fight. The other guy was a scout or sniper or some shit like that. They still use him on secret shit, I think."

Mad Dog said, "You bring up the rear when we get on patrol. I have a feeling I am point man. If we get separated, get these guys out. I'm going to talk to the radio man a second."

Mad Dog walked over to the radio man, a Marine named Collins, and said to him, "You got an extra list of frequencies in case you buy the farm and we have to use the radio?"

Collins handed Mad Dog a small package wrapped in plastic and said, "Dog, here they are for you."

Mad Dog, refusing the package said, "Give it to Charles. I think I'm point."

Collins came back, "No sergeants are points."

"You don't know Fenig," Mad Dog replied. "Better make sure Charles knows what to do if you can't use the radio. In fact, show the other guy too."

Turning to the third Marine, Mad Dog said, "What's your name?"

"Benson," the Marine replied. Dog walked over to the radio operator who began to show Benson and Charles the basics of the radio.

Fenig approached in a few minutes with Captain Wilson. Fenig immediately started orating. The C.O. knew beyond a shadow of a doubt that Fenig had bullshitted him, and wished silently that he hadn't given this assignment to him. The C.O. interrupted Fenig and said, "It's time to move out. Good luck.

Remember you're snooping, and not on S and D patrol, so avoid firefights."

With that they boarded the choppers. After they landed and were into the jungle Fenig ordered, "Dog, you take the point."

Bensen got behind Dog, then Collins, then Fenig with Charles in the rear, just like Mad Dog had wanted, if he had to go at all. The patrol moved through the jungle for only a brief period of time before the lieutenant ordered a halt to the patrol.

Fenig said, "We'll stay here for the night and move out at first light." The Marines settled in quickly. This was a blessing since they immediately heard Vietnamese chatter. The N.V.A. came within a few feet of them and seemed to be looking into the fields where the Marines had entered the jungle.

Mad Dog felt a tap on his arm and turned to see Fenig who said, "We're going to move. It's too dangerous here."

Mad Dog said, "Lieutenant, they're looking for us. They must have seen us land and maybe even saw us leave headquarters. We'd be better off to stay put and not move around. They may think that we are an ambush patrol because we've been sending them out from headquarters."

"I'm in charge," Fenig said. "Now move out, Sergeant, or I'll write you up for cowardliness."

The other three Marines looked at each other in shock and disbelief. All three now wished that they hadn't volunteered for this assignment.

Mad Dog got up and headed the way the N.V.A. patrol had come from. He went a short distance and stopped. When the five Marines were all together Mad Dog said, "Lieutenant, we could be walking into an ambush ourselves. This is a trick they use. They send three or four men out as bait and then set up an ambush if we don't bite."

The lieutenant was outraged and replied, "I'm in charge! Move out or so help me, I'll write you up and use these men as witnesses!" All three of the witnesses wanted to blow Fenig's head off, but Mad Dog turned and started to lead the patrol again.

Mad Dog stopped for no apparent reason—instincts, sixth sense, ESP, whatever you want to call it. He didn't have to stop the others. Benson saw Mad Dog stop, Collins saw Bensen, Fenig started to pass Collins when the night erupted in flame and noise. Mad Dog started to return fire and lob grenades. Benson, who was out of the field of fire of the N.V.A. ambush, started throwing grenades to protect Mad Dog. Charles ran past the lieutenant and Collins and threw two grenades. The firing stopped but the Marines could still hear the N.V.A. moving away from them in the jungle.

Charles, Benson and Collins ran to Mad Dog. Fenig stayed back. The Dog had the look of an insane person when the others saw his face. Charles and Collins said almost as if it were rehearsed, "Don't, Mad Dog! Don't!" They both knew he was ready to kill Fenig.

Fenig, who apparently grew some balls in the quiet moments, approached and said, "Okay men, let's get a body count to report."

It was all Mad Dog could do not to kill the arrogant lieutenant. "Fuck your body count, you fucking idiot! Our ass is compromised. We're on recon. Let's get our asses out of here!"

Fenig lost it. "That's it! You're on report, Sergeant! You're busted! You're private! You're nothing! I've got you now, big hero! You're ass is grass, you enlisted pig!"

It didn't help that all four of the Marines knew that it was said out of fear and Fenig was trying to cover it by attacking Mad Dog. Fenig pulled out his .45—which he hadn't done in the ambush—and declared, "Anyone who tries to go back to headquarters I'll shoot!"

Collins said, "Lieutenant, Mad Dog's right. We're on recon and we're compromised. Let's get the hell out of here!"

The lieutenant pointed his pistol at Collins and said, "One more word about retreat, and I'll kill you all!"

He had apparently gone over the edge.

The N.V.A. returned. One threw a grenade. Fortunately, it hit a tree branch and exploded to the side of the Marines. The Marines hit the deck and the N.V.A and Marines opened fire on one another. Fenig was up and running toward headquarters, the way they had come.

Mad Dog got Collin's grenades and yelled to Charles, "Get these guys back! I'll cover you and catch you at the clearing. Collins, start calling for choppers to get our asses out of here!"

Mad Dog began throwing grenades and firing his weapon on full automatic, then throwing another grenade and repeating the process. Finally he was totally out of ammunition and started to crawl away. He felt a sharp kick to his ribs and was looking at four AK-47's. Mad Dog looked up into the muzzles of the N.V.A. rifles. Almost instantly he felt a blow to the back of his head, saw red, then black and was unconscious.

He woke in a cage, stripped naked. Even his dog tags had been taken from him. His hands were bound behind his back. An N.V.A. officer approached the four guards at the cage. One of the guards unlocked it and Mad Dog was ordered out. He crawled out and was roughly jerked to his feet by two of the guards.

The officer spoke. "Ivan David Matthews, you are a murderer. You will answer all questions and confess your crime. Your Geneva Convention does not apply to criminals like you Americans. What is your battalion?"

Mad Dog said, "Fuck you, Jack!"

The N.V.A. kicked him in the groin and Mad Dog collapsed in a heap.

The N.V.A. officer said, "Perhaps you need more time to consider. We will not be so humane as in the past."

Thoughts of his men's fingernails pulled out and the burning of the Montagnard village flashed through his mind. "Humane!" he thought.

He was spread-eagled face down and any N.V.A. walking by sharply kicked him or lashed his back with a bamboo switch. They also used him for a urinal. Whenever any of them had to urinate they stood over his staked-out, whip-lashed, naked body and urinated on him. This went on all day.

As he lay there, the heat from the jungle grew more and more oppressive. It seemed that all the flies and gnats in the jungle swarmed around his body, biting and stinging him in the open wounds on his body. Fire ants crawled all over him, their bites stinging his flesh.

Mad Dog knew he was in trouble and that things were going to get much worse. He had no idea how much worse.

That evening he was roughly jerked over and his arms were tied behind his back. A pole, approximately four inches in diameter was shoved between his arms and back. He was then forced to his knees, kneeling before the North Vietnamese officer.

The N.V.A. officer spoke. "Speak now, bellhop. Yes, I know what you Marines are called. Jarhead, jungle bunny, sea bellhop. You cannot fool the great Vietnamese people, nor can you defeat us. Your own country is against you. Confess and you will be treated humanely, as we treat all of our prisoners, including criminals."

Mad Dog raised his head with some effort, looked the N.V.A. in the eyes, and said, "The only bell I ever hopped was your mamma and she was a bum fuck."

The N.V.A. officer wasn't quite sure what he had just been told. He took a step back, thought for a second, and then kicked Mad Dog in the stomach. Mad Dog again collapsed. He prayed for death silently while trying to get his breath.

The N.V.A. officer barked some orders and sneered at Mad Dog. "You will regret not giving me a confession. You will see. I will break you, Marine."

Mad Dog got his breath back. He was spread-eagled and staked out again. This time he was face up. Two N.V.A.s approached the four who had been left to guard him. The officer returned and urinated as best he could on Mad Dog's face. He then turned and nodded his head at the two latecomers.

They went to Mad Dog's feet. One had a bag with long, thin, sharply pointed bamboo stakes about as thick as a knitting needle. One N.V.A. got Mad Dog by each foot. The first rammed a spike under Mad Dog's big toe. Mad Dog screamed in pain. A few seconds later, after his body had recovered, the second N.V.A. rammed a spike through the bottom of Mad Dog's foot and pounded it all the way in up along his shin bone until the point came out from under the skin. Mad Dog's screams filled the jungle. This continued until all of Mad Dog's toes were impaled and he had two stakes rammed through each foot. The spikes in his toes were then jerked out. The ones through his feet were left in.

The rest of the night and all through the morning, anyone who walked by the cage stopped to lash his back, urinate on him, or jerk the stakes in his feet. He was not allowed to sleep. Every time he would look like he was losing consciousness, one of the men would jerk the stakes in his feet to bring him back to the awareness of the excruciating pain.

The next morning he was again pulled from the cage. His hands were jerked behind his back and tied. The bamboo pole was again shoved between his arms and his back and he was again forced to his knees, kneeling before the North Vietnamese officer. The officer said, "I warn you, speak to me now."

Against his own better judgment, blinded with pain, Mad Dog looked up at the officer so that he could look him squarely in the eyes and said, "Fuck you, you gook motherfucker."

The officer lashed out and smacked Mad Dog in the face. The man standing at the side of him grabbed his head and tilted it back. The officer spoke something to one of the other guards. The guard handed him his rifle. The officer took it in his hands and smashed the butt into Mad Dog's mouth. In a rage he hit him three or four times in the mouth with the butt of the heavy weapon.

Mad Dog was almost unconscious. His mouth was bloodied, his nose was shattered, his teeth broken. They still held his head backwards. When he began to recover, the officer smashed the rifle butt into the side of his face, breaking his cheekbone. He walked to the other side, smashed the other side. Then he hit him across the eyebrows with the butt of the weapon.

Mad Dog's face was unrecognizable. Cut and smashed from the butt of the rifle, his lips were swollen, his eyes were blackened, his face a bloody pulp. The pole was removed. He was laid out and staked again, face up this time. They took two rocks, and placed one under each hand, his fingers directly over the rocks.

Again the North Vietnamese officer walked over and sneered, "Talk nowww, Marine. Criminal, talk nowwwww . . . "

Although Mad Dog didn't know it, the officer was losing face, not being able to break him. Mad Dog's hand was moved so one finger was on top of the rock . . . the small finger of his right hand.

The officer walked around and snarled, "Speakkk!!!"

Mad Dog couldn't even think, let alone speak. He mouthed something.

The officer smiled and bent over and said, "Speak."

Mad Dog spit—a weak splatter of blood that barely touched the officer's face because of Mad Dog's weakened position. The officer, enraged again, jumped to his feet, grabbed the rifle and smashed it twice hard on Mad Dog's little finger, totally shattering it.

Mad Dog was in so much pain, he couldn't think, he couldn't speak.

The officer waited a few minutes, smashed the ring finger on Mad Dog's right hand.

This went on. The officer would wait until Mad Dog's senses were back, then smash with savage blows another finger on his right hand until all the fingers were mangled.

Then he waited a little longer, and grunted, "Speak to me now. Speak to me nowwww!!!" becoming enraged and desperate.

Mad Dog couldn't move, couldn't think. He wanted to scream. But he couldn't.

The officer again gave instructions.

Mad Dog's left hand was smashed. A finger at a time. Again there was waiting between each savage blow.

The officer again issued orders and Mad Dog was thrown back into the cage.

The gook officer wanted to kill Mad Dog, but now it was a matter of him saving face. He had predicted that he would make this Marine talk. And now, with each passing session, he lost more face. And face, to Orientals, is everything. He wanted so desperately just to put a bullet in Mad Dog's head, but he knew to keep the respect of his superiors and the men under him, that he had to break Mad Dog.

Mad Dog was shackled to a steel pin in the floor. He was barely alive, barely able to think. He lay on his back looking through the bars of his cage at the jungle canopy and the sunlight shining through. He whispered aloud while uncontrollably crying in agony, "God, I know that I am not exactly a great person but I never asked you to make me brave, a hero, or to give me medals. Please God, please don't let me be a disgrace to you, or the USA, or the Corps. Please God, let me die."

Blinded by pain, he passed out.

THE RESCUE

The three Marines made it to the edge of the jungle. Collins had called for a rescue chopper that they could hear coming in the distance. Cowering in the jungle cover was Fenig, pistol still drawn. Collins tried to get him to put it away.

"Where's Mad Dog?" Fenig asked.

Collins answered, "We think he bought the farm. He covered our get away."

Fenig smiled his insane smile and holstered his pistol.

When they got back to headquarters, Captain Wilson was waiting with a group of officers including a full colonel from headquarters.

"What happened?" Captain Wilson asked.

Fenig said, "I tried to save Sergeant Matthews but couldn't. He disobeyed my orders."

"You lying motherfucker, Lieutenant! You ran away and left us all to protect your ass! The Dog stayed to cover us. If it wasn't for him we would all be dead except for you. We should'a let him kill your white bread ass, motherfucker. Now you bust my ass down to private like you done the Dog when he tried to tell you we all should get out of there!"

Charles' eyes were bulging and he was ready to kill Fenig.

The colonel stepped forward and said, "Captain Wilson, separate these three Marines. I want a complete report from each of them. As soon as they're completed, get them to me on the double."

As some staff N.C.O.s stepped forward to take the three Marines to separate locations, Collins said, "Colonel, sir, Lieutenant Fenig threatened to shoot me. I don't trust him with a weapon."

"Captain Wilson," the colonel said, "disarm all four of the Marines and have each one escorted until I have the reports."

Captain Wilson knew that disarming them all was only done to appease any sense of protocol in having to disarm an officer. The C.O. looked at Fenig with disgust that he could not disguise. Fenig was already calculating his alibi, and letting his megalomania take over to make him feel above these mere mortals.

Colonel Tartus, as battalion commanding officer, had jurisdiction in the matter. Colonel Fike, who had requested the reports, recommended to Colonel Tartus that Fenig be disciplined severely, but not wanting to seem dictatorial, did not make specific recommendations. Tartus, in his quest to keep everyone happy, sent Fenig to Da Nang and made an informal request that Fenig not be allowed to lead troops in combat. No disciplinary action of any kind was ever taken.

The next day in camp . . .

Oop had returned from R and R with booze for everyone. The new C.O. gave him the bad news of Mad Dog's supposed death.

Oop sat down almost as in a trance.

"Captain, I request permission to speak to the survivors."

"I'll get them on the double, Gunny," the captain said. "Get the men from last night's patrol in here, Corporal."

When they all assembled in the captain's tent, Oop spoke. "Did any of you actually see Sergeant Matthews killed or captured?"

Charles replied first, "If Matthews is Mad Dog's real name, no, we didn't."

Collins added, "Gunny, we were running for our lives! That fuckin' lieutenant almost got us all waxed. Mad Dog saved our asses!"

Benson said, "Gunny, if there is going to be a recon to see if the Dog is alive, or to recover his body, I volunteer to go. I know right where we left him."

Charles and Collins immediately volunteered to go also.

Oop turned to the captain.

"Sir, request permission to recon the area to see if we can find any sign of Sergeant Matthews."

Captain Wilson said, "I'll get on it right now," and called for his radio man to get the colonel on the horn.

Colonel Tartus was not receptive to the idea of another recon patrol in the same area. Captain Wilson showed his mettle when he said, "Colonel Tartus, request permission to speak to Colonel Fike."

Tartus said, "I'll get back to you, Captain."

He knew his career would be over, but Wilson was known as a leader, and had won the respect of his troops and superiors wherever he had commanded men. He knew that he had to take a stand now and not blame anyone . . . just do what had to be done.

"Colonel Fike, I need a decision quickly. Gunny Clarke is here with the men from last night's patrol and they feel that there is a chance that Sergeant Matthews may be alive. I want to send a recon patrol to check it out and I need authorization. Colonel Tartus is too busy to make a decision now!"

The colonel ok'd the patrol and ordered the captain to have his company ready to move out on choppers if the recon patrol needed assistance. He changed his mind aloud and said, "We better have the entire battalion ready. I'll take care of it. Get the patrol moving!"

Oop's plan was to find out if Mad Dog was alive, then call in air strikes and artillery. The recon squad approached the area from a totally different direction than the previous night. They had plotted in advance their path to the place where Mad Dog was seen, as they wanted it to appear that they were headed to a different area. The squad moved as quickly as possible through the night to the place where the ambush had taken place. They silently searched, but found no trace of Mad Dog.

They took cover and settled in for the night. N.V.A. patrols walked within a few feet of them several times during the night but they remained undiscovered. Oop decided to check the area later in the day. He felt there would be too much activity in the morning.

Shortly before noon the Marines started to move in the direction that the previous night's patrols had come from. The clearing came upon them so fast that the point man almost walked into it before he knew what he was doing. There, in the center of the clearing, was a cage with four guards around it. They were taking turns beating whoever was in the cage with bamboo sticks.

Oop looked through his binoculars. Almost unrecognizable was Mad Dog. The guards on the cage were the only activity in the camp. Every time that Mad Dog's eyes closed they jabbed him or smacked him with their sticks or did something to his feet.

Oop knew there would be no way to get to him with the small patrol. He radioed headquarters and asked for an airborne assault. He assigned two men to shoot each guard around Mad Dog the minute the assault started. He assigned two others to rescue Mad Dog. Oop then asked for artillery fire to the right of the N.V.A. camp. This was the best landing spot for the airborne assault.

Captain Wilson had been waiting by the radio all night and day for any report from his men. This officer was a Marine! As soon as all was set and in order, he joined his company for the mission at hand. The choppers lifted off with the combat-ready Marines. The artillery fire was timed to end as the choppers were ready to land. The choppers flew parallel to the artillery barrage then swooped in and out of the sun in hopes that the artillery fire had bought them some time.

Colonel Fike went to the communications shack and stood by to direct any assistance needed on this operation. The radio man was amazed but the colonel looked at him and said, "Son, we're getting one of ours back one way or another, and if me being here helps, this is where I belong."

The artillery barrage hit some fuel and ammo dumps that the Marines had not seen to the rear of the camp. Simultaneously Oop's sharpshooters blew away the four guards around the cage. As the choppers landed, Oop and Mad Dog's two rescuers dashed to the cage. The door had a steel chain and a lock holding it shut, but luckily they had brought bolt cutters with them.

Mad Dog was shackled to a pin in the ground. The two Marines crawled into the cage to cut him loose and ease him out. He was such a sickening sight that if the adrenaline had not been flowing, the rescuers would have become ill.

His toenails, from the bamboo spikes, were torn loose and hanging by shreds. There were two spikes that had been pounded through the bottom of each foot sticking out the bottoms of his feet and the sides of his shins. His face was beaten in, his smashed hands were bleeding and swollen, and the welts on his back and legs, covered with flies, were oozing and bleeding from the whippings. He reeked of urine. Mad Dog couldn't move.

Captain Wilson had wisely assigned four men to be stretcher-bearers. He ran to the cage where Mad Dog was being eased out. He said, "We got a stretcher. Let's get him out, on a chopper and the fucking hell out of here!"

Carefully yet quickly the Marines got Mad Dog on the stretcher and rushed to a waiting medevac chopper that whisked him away to the field hospital. Mad Dog was in so much pain that he could not even blink at his rescuers.

The remaining Marines kicked ass and took names. A large cache of supplies was found and destroyed. The battalion of Marines had routed a division of N.V.A.s. Mad Dog was treated at the field hospital and flown quickly to a hospital ship. When he sufficiently recovered he was flown to a naval hospital in Yokusaka, Japan for major repairs and therapy. Everyone now had Mad Dog's story.

Mad Dog asked over and over, "Why did they risk everyone for me?" He just wanted to be repaired and sent back to combat, his home.

THE RAIN

The company had minor duties and certain areas to guard. It was routine and boring, but they needed a respite from the constant on-the-edge alertness that was required in the field. An occasional probe of three or four N.V.A.s or a few mortar rounds lobbed into camp were really just enough to keep the men from being too relaxed.

One of the replacements, Staff Sergeant Post, often said that he was, quote, "the Dog's replacement."

The men and officers didn't find this humorous, and Oop tried to guide him, but to no avail. "Post, Mad Dog had the respect of every man in this company and probably battalion. You're not going to help yourself get settled in with these guys by comparing yourself to the Dog."

"I outrank these guys," was his reply. "They'll just have to get adjusted to me. Lieutenant Fenig told me in Da Nang that Mad Dog was a shit bird."

Oop fought to control himself as his hands stiffened and he spoke through clenched teeth. "Post, Fenig is a fuckin' idiot that got more men in this company killed than the gooks did by their own means. If Fenig is your mentor, you're going to have a rocky road from the troops and ninety nine percent of the officers and staff N.C.O.s as well."

Post took this in with a stupid shit-eating grin on his face and walked away.

For night guard duty usually a squad went to its sector and spent the night, being relieved in the morning. Sergeant Post, who wasn't needed or wanted, prepared to go with one squad. He got all decked out in his combat gear, full pack and all the trimmings, including crossed bandoleers of ammunition across his chest. He also had a 35mm camera, so the men could take pictures of this magnificent warrior.

Corporal Carl, who normally was in charge, was especially resentful of Post, since Mad Dog had actually saved his life. Carl spoke to the squad, "Hey guys, this asshole Post is all dressed out for a two-week S and D, complete with cam—er—a!!! We're going to cooperate taking his pictures, but we're going to fuck up the background! Got me?"

In unison the squad replied in the affirmative.

"Carl, have somebody come here so I can show them how to use my camera. I want some pictures taken," Post called.

"Oh yes, Massa. Does you wants a white boy or is a wet back or one of my Niggers okay?"

The men almost blew the plan as they started to snicker.

Post grandiosely replied, "Anybody trainable will do."

Carl called to Lipford, an innocent looking baby-faced Marine, who in fact was wilder and woollier than most, but usually escaped punishment because of his sweet demeanor and looks. Lipford went charging to Post.

"Thank you for letting me do this, Sarge!"

Post smiled and whispered, "We gotta stick together, right?"

"Oh, yes sir!" nodded Lipford, convincing Post that he was on his side.

Post went through various poses and what he thought were "combat" contortions. The men, wise in the way of screwing up people, spread out in the background for each shot. Every photo taken included a Marine pissing, or attempting to crap or giving the finger. The gang back at Post's home town got a real view of combat.

One night, several weeks later, the N.V.A. on a probe got a few of their men inside and caused some minor problems until they were captured. The Marines on guard were naturally keyed up, and were told not to move around, so that the patrols looking for the N.V.A. would not fire on their own men.

It started raining and the men wrapped themselves in their ponchos to prepare for a miserable, cold wet night. Post had rigged up an idiotic, elaborate, stupid plan to keep dry to show the men that he was an intelligent Marine. (Of course, he had never been in the field, or he would have known that the bare minimum is what's called for. On patrol, day after day, two pounds sometimes seemed like a hundred.)

"Corporal," he ordered, "I want you to inflate this here air mattress."

Corporal Carl said, "Hey, Sergeant, that's personal servitude. It ain't allowed. We ain't your fuckin' slaves!"

Post cursed and began huffing and puffing to inflate the air mattress. Then he laid it down, got on it and covered himself totally, including his face.

"You guys are a bunch of dick heads! None of you guys were smart enough to think of this! You'll all get soaking wet, and I'll be high and dry," he said to no one in particular.

Some small arms fire erupted to the right of their position. One of the men shook Post, "Hey, there's incoming small arms."

He said, "Don't touch me, I'm awake."

Just then three N.V.A.s jumped up directly in front of the position. The Marines reacted. One N.V.A. had thrown a grenade. The Marines cut two of them down, the third broke through and bayoneted Post who had never moved. The Marines riddled the N.V.A. with bullets, but it was too late for Post. He was gurgling.

Carl pulled down the poncho covering Post's face. Post had a look, not of pain, but of surprise. His lips moved, but he never uttered another sound.

The grenade had severely wounded one of the young Marines. The corpsman got to him, took one look and backed off and shook his head no.

Carl and Martinez prayed with the youngster in their arms. Carl said, "Can we do anything, man?"

The dying young man said, "Let's sing Christmas carols." The Marines looked at each other, and started to sing Christmas carols in the October rain.

The young Marine went to be with God with the odd blend of Marines not really knowing the tune or the words trying to sing "It Came Upon a Midnight Clear."

The rain continued to fall.

OOP

Oop was leading a patrol along the ridge. There was a stream below and in the distance a Vietnamese village. Oop radioed headquarters.

"Boxer, this is Boxer 44. Over."

"This is Boxer. Go ahead. Over."

"We're at check point three, about a half click from the zip village. Over."

"Boxer 44, this is Boxer. Move down and check out the vill. We have alerted the arty battery of your location. If you need help they're on standby. Over."

"This is 44. Roger. Out."

As the patrol started down the side of the ridge to the village, a shot rang out. No one was sure where it hit, but Oop called in a few rounds of artillery to the side of the village toward the river.

The first rounds opened up huge tunnels that were leading from the river to the village. Oop's radio man instinctively raised headquarters and handed Oop the hand set.

"The arty blew open some tunnels from the river to the vill. Over."

"Check them out. Reinforcements are on the way. Over."

Oop answered, "Roger. Out."

"Spread out! Let's sweep the vill all the way to the river."

As the patrol approached the village, eight women, five of them pregnant, ran out and locked arms across the trail leading to the village. Before thinking, one of the men stepped off the trail to go around the women. A shot rang out. He had stepped on a booby trap that fires one shot into the groin of whoever sets it off. The Marine crumpled in pain.

Another Marine yelled, "Corpsman, corpsman!"

Oop shouted, "Don't get off the trail!"

But in the confusion the corpsman ran off the side of the trail and set off a "bouncing Betty," a booby trap designed to go about five feet high and blow off a man's head. The explosion killed the corpsman and gave wounds to three other Marines.

While this was going on, armed Vietnamese were seen running towards the river. Corporal Carl, who had been with the company when the Marines' throats had been slit, ran up and pushed the women out of the way and without any orders, the fire team took them as prisoners.

Oop called for a medevac chopper for the wounded and a chopper for the prisoners. The patrol ran to the river where the men with the weapons had run.

When they got to the river, several small tunnel openings were found. When Oop got to where his men had found the tunnels, he yelled, "Tunnel Rat, get your ass up here and earn your pay!"

A Marine, small in stature, came running on the double and was taking off his pack even before Oop was able to give him instructions.

Oop said to the tunnel rat, "Grebosky, take it slow and easy. They may have snakes tied along the tunnel. I want you to back out at the first problem you see or pull the line and we'll pull you out."

Grebosky had joined the Marine Corps with the idea of being a tunnel rat, and this was the first opportunity to practice what he had trained for. Grebosky was tied to the line and started into the tunnel. The tunnel rat had a powerful flashlight attached to a stick three feet long. He was only in the tunnel about ten feet when he spotted movement. He turned the light to where he saw it, and crawled forward to where the flashlight lay so he could see what had moved. The North Vietnamese had tied deadly krait snakes to the side of the tunnel. Grebosky reached back to unsheathe his machete. After a few unsuccessful attempts, he cut the snakes in two.

He continued to keep the parts with the heads attached away from his hands with the machete. After agonizing minutes, he had the huge knife on one head and in a sawing motion split it open and brushed it to the side. He worked his way to the other head and did the same. He then pushed the flashlight contraption ahead as the tunnel turned to the left.

A burst of automatic weapon fire filled the tunnel. Dust and dirt flew and engulfed him. The light had been hit. Grebosky was in total darkness. He calmed himself and reached to his side for a smaller spare flashlight. He crept forward in the darkness so that he could see around the curve.

When he had his light in place, he held the line in his hand and pulled on it to be hauled backwards as he flipped on the light. He tried to see what he could. As he was pulled backward, the tunnel rat got a view of what looked like a large chamber. Again automatic weapons fire filled the tunnel with bullets, noise, dust and dirt.

"I got a glimpse of a big room. I couldn't see much else. I'm ready to go back in if you want me to," he reported to Oop when he got out of the tunnel.

"Can you estimate where you saw the room?"

Grebosky looked over the surface, walked to a spot about fifty feet away and said, "About here, Gunny."

"All right. A couple of you guys get out your entrenching tools and dig me some holes," Oop ordered.

Three men quickly helped each other get their entrenching tools off their packs and started digging in the rocky ground.

"First squad get to the holes on the river bank. Second squad and the walking wounded, watch the prisoners.The rest of you spread out in fire teams and keep your eyes open."

Oop then placed explosives in the holes his men had dug. The first explosions didn't do much except make the holes in the ground bigger. The next charges were put into place and Oop had them covered with more dirt. This time slight holes were made through to the cave. Oop popped a grenade into the largest of the holes. The explosion was muffled by the earth.

"Minh," Oop called to his interpreter, "tell them to come out now or we're going to put more explosives into their tunnel."

The interpreter yelled into the hole. There was no response.

Just then the choppers started to arrive. Captain Wilson got off with the rest of the company and a crew of engineers. The wounded Marines were medevaced and the prisoners taken away.

Captain Wilson asked Oop, "What's happening, Gunny?"

"There's three tunnel openings at the river and Grebosky located what looks to be an underground storage room. I popped a couple grenades in it and had Minh tell them to come out."

One of the engineers said, "Good job, Gunny! Let's see if we can get them out."

The engineers went to the tunnel opening and the hole Oop had blasted in the ground. They dropped tear gas canisters into the opening and immediately covered the holes with plastic to keep the fumes in. Then they went to the tunnel openings, put small explosive charges in them and blew them up to seal them off.

The N.V.A. started to emerge at the openings to the village. The waiting Marines promptly took them captive. The prisoners were then loaded aboard trucks which had also arrived in the interim and were taken to camps for interrogation and internment.

FINAL

Rainy season came. It was incredible that it could be cold in 80° weather. For a long time it was 120° in the shade, and the men got accustomed to it. The next day when it rained they were shivering as though they were at the North Pole in their skivvy drawers.

Scuttlebutt had it that the action would taper off in the rainy season. It was a relief to some and a disappointment to others, as always. Captain Wilson's company was given orders to return to Dong Ha. They would be getting a breather to replace the equipment and men they had lost. His men were actually going to sleep on cots, in tents! Compared to what they were used to, this was the Marriott!

No one had heard from Mad Dog since he had been medevaced six weeks prior. Imagine the surprise when Mad Dog came limping on two crutches through the tents. He had finagled a route through Vietnam to say "Hi" and farewell to his buddies.

Oop spotted him from one side and Corporal Carl spotted him from his tent. They both rushed to him and tried to assist him. It was awkward as always for a few seconds, because after all, Marines don't cry or hug each other. They both wanted to support him, and help him walk. But after several awkward attempts, they decided they would do him less harm to let him walk with his crutches himself.

Captain Wilson came out of his tent and invited them inside. He knew that he was in the presence of greatness, the legendary Mad Dog. He said, "Mad Dog, I consider it a privilege to have served with you in combat. Even if you had only done one tenth of what we know you've done, you'd still be one of the greatest Marines ever. Sometimes I just can't believe what you did and how you did it, even though I saw it with my own eyes."

He broke out a bottle, handed it to Mad Dog and said, "Pass it around."

He turned to Mad Dog and asked, "Mad Dog, is there anyone else you'd like to see?"

Mad Dog replied, "Yes sir, Captain. I'd like to see my men. I'd also like to see the men that were on the patrol with me. To tell you the truth, Captain, I wish I could shake everybody's hand! I never really thought I was worth the battalion taking a chance on losing a lot of men to save me. Every time I think of it, I get so humbled." His voice trailed off. "I just don't understand . . . "

Captain Wilson didn't have to give any orders. One of the other sergeants who had been there, left to get the other two men who had been on the patrol, and Captain Wilson said that they would escort Mad Dog to all the tents so that he could see at least all the men in the company.

Oop and Carl escorted Mad Dog to the tent where most of his men were. Carl ran to the others to tell the rest of the men that Mad Dog was back. The Marines were in awe. Mad Dog thanked them and said, "You do me proud, guys. I never knew what a Marine was till I met you. Thanks a lot. I hope God blesses every one of you."

As he was getting up to leave, the general, his aide, and several officers approached and entered the tent.

One of the men yelled, "Ten-hut!"

The general said, "As you were." He walked over to Mad Dog. "I stand at attention to you, Marine! When I get disgusted with what I read about young Americans and wonder what we are raising, I think of you, and I know that we bring up smarter, stronger, braver Marines!"

He extended his hand. As Mad Dog reached to take it, the general, who was much taller than Mad Dog, threw his arms around him.

The Marines applauded and cheered and the entire company walked back to the airstrip with Mad Dog, every man giving him encouragement and touching his heart.

Mad Dog boarded the C-130 and it flew off into the evening sky to Da Nang where he would catch his jet back to the land of the big PX, the world, and to the pain and heartbreak that accompanies a warrior whose country has rejected the men who did battle in her name . . . nobody's warriors.